The Future of Social Movements in Canada

S.D. Clark

The University of Toronto's Department of Sociology was established in 1963. Samuel Delbert (S.D.) Clark (1910–2003) was its founding chair.

Clark was born in Lloydminster, Alberta, and attended the University of Saskatchewan, the London School of Economics, McGill University and the University of Toronto. He analyzed the transformation of successive Canadian frontiers from socially disorganized settlements into organized societies. He then conducted research on how economic change in Canada resulted in inequality as reflected in patterns of residential segregation. His books include *The Canadian Manufacturers Association* (1939), *The Social Development of Canada* (1942), *Church and Sect in Canada* (1948), *Movements of Political Protest in Canada* (1959), *The Developing Canadian Community* (1962), *The Suburban Society* (1966), *Canadian Society in Historical Perspective* (1976) and *The New Urban Poor* (1978).

Clark served as president of the Canadian Political Science Association, honorary president of the Canadian Sociology and Anthropology Association and president of the Royal Society of Canada. He was awarded the J.B. Tyrell Historical Medal, became a foreign honorary member of the American Academy of Arts and Sciences and an Officer of the Order of Canada, and received honorary degrees from half a dozen Canadian universities.

In 1999, Clark's son, William Edmund (Ed) Clark, endowed the S.D. Clark Chair in Sociology at the University of Toronto in honour of his father.

The Future of Social Movements in Canada

PROCEEDINGS OF THE FOURTH
S.D. CLARK SYMPOSIUM
ON THE FUTURE OF CANADIAN SOCIETY

EDITED BY
Robert Brym

Rock's Mills Press
Oakville, Ontario
2019

PUBLISHED BY

ROCK'S MILLS PRESS
www.rocksmillspress.com

Cover Photo: The Indignants/Flickr. *Idle No More is a social movement that was launched in December 2012. It promoted Indigenous sovereignty to protect water, air, and land. The layering of a single strong colour over a black-and-white photo was a technique first employed by the Blue Note jazz label in the 1940s and 1950s, when jazz was strongly associated with the struggle for equality by Black Americans. It is a style that is appropriately invoked for the subject of this book.*

For information, contact customer.service@rocksmillspress.com.
Library and Archives Canada Cataloguing in Publication data is available from the publisher.

Contents

List of Figures

List of Tables

The Future of
Social Movements
in Canada

CHAPTER ONE

The Future of Social Movements in Canada: An Introduction

Robert Brym

Declinism Rises

In 1918, German historian Oswald Spengler (1918–22 [1927]) published the first volume of *The Decline of the West*. It became a bestseller among members of the educated class. Surveying human history, Spengler argued that civilizations rise and decline in thousand-year cycles. At its height, each civilization enjoys a unifying idea, a deep sense of tradition, and a distinct and respected hierarchy of authority. In decline, the unifying idea weakens, the sense of tradition is lost, and the hierarchy of authority is called into question. According to Spengler, the West entered such a period of decline in the late nineteenth century. He expected it to collapse around the year 2000.

The feeling today is that Spengler may have been on to something. The academic field of what might be called "declinism" has become a growth industry. Books and articles on the subject seem to be published almost weekly. The "winter of despair" to which Dickens alluded in the opening lines of *A Tale of Two Cities* seems to be upon us, and although some stubborn optimists believe, as Dickens wrote, that we are "all going direct to Heaven," it is considerably more fashionable in academic circles to claim, again quoting Dickens, that we are "all going direct the other way" (Dickens 1859).

Much of the anguish focuses on the crisis of democracy due to the rise of right-wing, nativist, pro-capitalist movements and regimes (often vaguely called "populist") headed by Trump in the United States, Orban in Hungary, Conte in Italy, Erdogan in Turkey, Dutarte in the Philippines, Bolsonaro in Brazil, and others. Accordingly, it is useful to place the current crisis of democracy in historical perspective.

Democracy Cycles

Phase 1 of the story begins in 1828, when most white men in the United States were permitted to vote in that year's presidential election (see Figure 1.1). For nearly a century after that, the franchise was broadened geographically and socially, typically under pressure from social movements, notably the labour, suffragette, and civil rights movements. Although racial exclusion persisted in most jurisdictions, property ownership requirements were gradually reduced or eliminated as a condition for exercising the franchise. The first female members of parliament were elected in Finland in 1907. A decade later, the first Canadian women were permitted to vote. By 1921, the United States, most of Western Europe, the British Dominions, and four Latin American countries were at least minimally democratic.

Figure 1.1. Democratic cycles since 1828

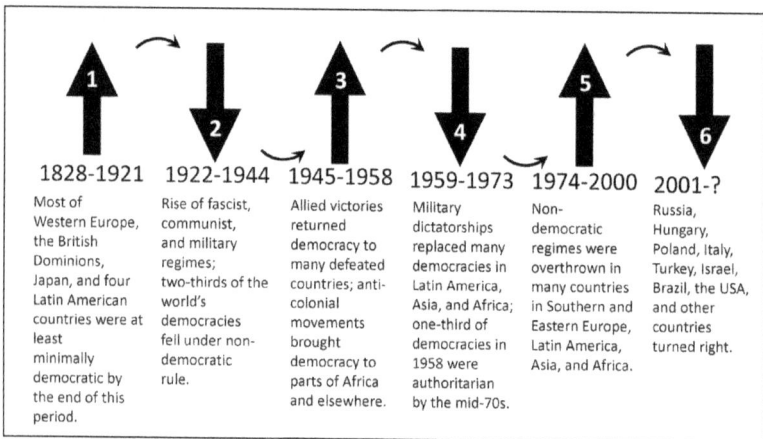

1828-1921	1922-1944	1945-1958	1959-1973	1974-2000	2001-?
Most of Western Europe, the British Dominions, Japan, and four Latin American countries were at least minimally democratic by the end of this period.	Rise of fascist, communist, and military regimes; two-thirds of the world's democracies fell under non-democratic rule.	Allied victories returned democracy to many defeated countries; anti-colonial movements brought democracy to parts of Africa and elsewhere.	Military dictatorships replaced many democracies in Latin America, Asia, and Africa; one-third of democracies in 1958 were authoritarian by the mid-70s.	Non-democratic regimes were overthrown in many countries in Southern and Eastern Europe, Latin America, Asia, and Africa.	Russia, Hungary, Poland, Italy, Turkey, Israel, Brazil, the USA, and other countries turned right.

Sources: Adapted from Huntington (1991); Diamond (1996).

The first, 93-year-long phase of democratization ended abruptly in 1922, when the fascist blackshirt movement organized a mass demonstration in Rome, and Mussolini became Italy's leader. Stalin came to power in 1924 and Hitler in 1933. By 1942, two-thirds of the world's democracies had fallen under fascist or communist rule.

Phase 3 began when Allied victory in World War II returned democracy to many defeated countries, and anti-colonial movements brought democracy to Algeria, Tunisia, Morocco, Ghana, India, Burma, South Korea, and Indonesia.

However, just as an undertow begins when an ocean wave recedes, another democratic reversal began in 1959. In phase 4, military dictatorships took control of many countries in Southern and Eastern Europe, Latin America, Asia, and Africa. One-third of the world's democracies in 1958 were authoritarian regimes by the mid-1970s.

Portugal's peaceful Carnation Revolution in 1974 marked the beginning of phase 5; an unexpected movement of civil resistance brought democracy back to the country, and Portugal withdrew from its African colonies. From 1974 to the end of the twentieth century, Spain, Greece, the entire Soviet bloc, Brazil, Argentina, and a whole series of countries in Africa and Asia were swept up in the biggest democratic wave ever. Social movements were the prime movers.

Finally, as the twenty-first century dawned, the democratic wave receded, and the current malaise began.

The picture that emerges from this overview is not Spenglerian, but it is cyclical. After the first 93 years of democratization, we find that every democratic retrenchment was followed by a democratic resurgence, each phase of the cycle lasting about 15 to 25 years. This means that Marx (1847) was only half right when he observed that "it is the bad side that produces the movement ... by providing a struggle." What he neglected to observe is that it is the good side that produces the counter-movement by providing a struggle.

Ignoring cyclicality, what is democracy's overall linear trend, if any? Figure 1.2 covers the last democratic cycle, phases 5 and 6. It is based on the Freedom House index, which awards countries points based on the scope and effectiveness of political and personal rights and freedoms enjoyed by their citizens. The index ranges from 0 to 100, with high scores indicating more freedom. After scores are awarded, cut-offs are established, and countries are sorted into three groups: *unfree* countries like Russia and Saudi Arabia, *partly free* countries like Mexico, and *free* countries like Canada and the United States. Free countries are liberal democracies that enjoy a separation

Figure 1.2. Liberal democracies and other regime types as percent of all countries, 1972–2017

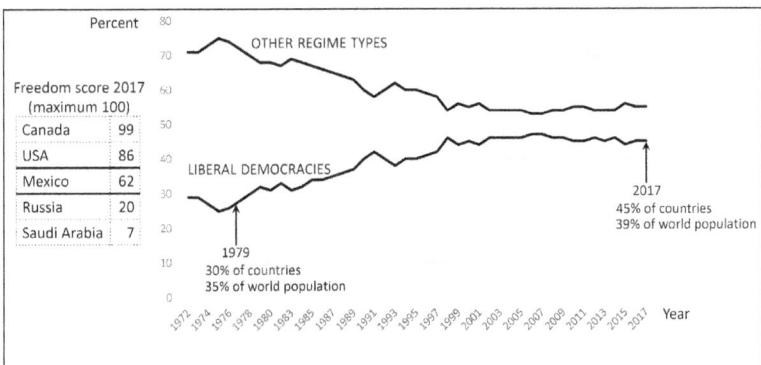

Sources: Adapted from Gastil (1979); Freedom House (2018).

of powers, checks and balances, a free press, and protection of minority rights, although they do so to varying degrees, as indicated by the 13-point difference in 2017 between Canada and the United States, both liberal democracies.

Figure 2.2 also shows how liberal democracy has fared since Freedom House started collecting data in 1972. The graph shows the number of liberal democracies and other regime types in the world as a percentage of all countries. The democratic surge of 1974–2000 appears clearly. But perhaps surprisingly, Figure 2.2 indicates stability, not decline, in the percentage of liberal-democratic regimes from 1997 to 2017. To date, the democratic crisis through which we are living has put a halt to the democratic surge of the late twentieth century and has resulted in attacks on democratic freedoms in many countries. However, it has evidently not caused a diminution in the number of liberal-democratic countries or the percentage of the world's population living in liberal democracies. This time, the democratic reversal is not as deep as it was in previous periods of retrenchment—at least, it wasn't as of 2017.

Solidarity Liquifies

To a degree, the story I've been telling is partly a story of military coups and wars. But it is also a story about social movements. For nearly two centuries, social movements have been prime movers in both democratic surges and retrenchments.

If we zoom out a little further, allowing our lens to encompass most of Spengler's thousand years rather than just the last two centuries, we discover a second important feature of social movements. The structure and aims of movements have changed in tandem with the overarching political structures in which they are embedded (see Table 1.1).

As Charles Tilly and Lesley Wood (2004 [2013]) note, before the era of modern states, collective contention was typically small, localized, violent, and transient, like the 1358 uprising in the Beauvais region of France. According to a chronicler of that event—and leaving aside the provocation that prompted a leaderless group of men to act—one member of the group proclaimed that the French nobility were a disgrace to the realm and should be destroyed. His comrades shouted, "He's right!" and they went off with their pikes and knives to a nearby castle, killed the knight, his wife, and their children, threw their bodies over the ramparts, and set fire to the place (Froissart c. 1365). Such episodic forms of collective contention were typical of the period.

Table 1.1. How power structures influence movements

Pre-1768: Transience	1768–1974: Solidarity	1975–?: Liquidity
Before the establishment of modern states, social movements were small, localized, violent, and short-lived.	Movements grew due to urbanization and industrialization; states drew the attention of movements to national issues; movements become bureaucratized and enduring.	Globalization helped to undermined solidarity among old movements but enabled digitized networks and drew the attention of new movements to global issues.

Source: Adapted from Tilly and Wood (2004 [2013]).

What we now recognize as the modern social movement first emerged only in the second half of the 18th century, the anti-slavery movement being the first of its kind. Modern states were forming. Each imposed a national language, a flag, an anthem, and conscription on its citizens, irrespective of ethnic and religious diversity, and taxed them at ever higher rates. Moreover, urbanization and industrialization brought many thousands of increasingly literate workers together in neighbourhoods, mines, and factories. Consequently, collective contention came to involve many more people than in earlier times. It became more bureaucratized and less episodic. And because the state made growing demands on the citizenry, the citizenry made more claims against national governments as opposed to local authorities. This was the era of organized social movement solidarity on a largely national scale.

At least one important movement, the communist movement, was decidedly international in scope during the era of solidarity. However, communism was heavily state-sponsored. The non-communist labour movement remained chiefly national in scope, and it fell on hard times beginning in the early 1970s, as figures on union density and strike activity from many countries demonstrate. Consider only the pattern of strike activity in Canada. One of the world's most strike-prone countries in 1974, Canada became largely pacified in this regard in the following decades (see Figure 1.3).

The pacification of the non-communist labour movement was largely the result of globalization. Beginning in the mid-1970s, barriers to foreign investment were lowered. As a result, more investment capital began flowing to low-wage jurisdictions, allowing profitability to increase. In North America, the downside was that factories started shutting down, and competition for capital investment started heating up. To retain jobs, North American govern-

Figure 1.3. Strikes per 100,000 non-agricultural workers, Canada, 1946–2017

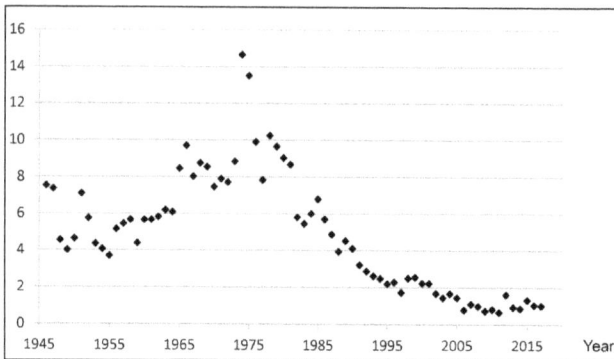

Sources: Brym, Birdsell-Bauer, and McIvor (2013); Statistics Canada (2018); Meltz (1976); Denton (1976a, 1976b, 1976c).

ments offered tax concessions to corporations and limited the ability of labour to win higher wages and improved welfare benefits. As the resources available to the labour movement declined, strike frequency followed suit, as did union density. In Canada, the percentage of unionized non-agricultural workers dropped 17 percent from 1974 to 2017 (calculated from Statistics Canada 2014; Statista 2018). The comparable figure for the United States was 54 percent (calculated from Bureau of Labor Statistics 2018; Mayer 2004). The era of nationally organized social movement solidarity waned.

Rapid increase in the speed and affordability of communication since the 1980s is an important part of the story of globalization. The Internet and cell phones have had profound implications for social movements because they have enabled people to exchange information and form bonds of association based on shared discontent, not much encumbered by considerations of cost, time, and space. In 2011–12, the Arab Spring, Occupy, Idle No More, and other movements, many of them transnational in scope, surprised the world by targeting, propagandizing, recruiting, organizing, and mobilizing on a large scale via digital communications media. Some analysts, Manuel Castells (2012 [2015]) chief among them, proclaimed that a new era of social movement organization, based on horizontal digital networks, had been born. And they were right.

Whether such movements will have a lasting impact, as Castells and others believe, is a separate question (Slavina and Brym 2019). To date, the record is less than encouraging. The last occupation of the Occupy movement ended on 16 May 2012 in St. John's, Newfoundland and Labrador, just 152 days after the first occupation began in New York City. The long-term impact of the Occupy movement is ambiguous at best. It took only two years for the Arab Spring to turn into the Arab Winter.

Democracy seems increasingly fragile even in Tunisia, whose claim to be the Arab Spring's only success story is wearing thin (Andersen and Brym 2017; Brym and Andersen 2016; Daragahi 2018). Canada's Idle No More movement followed a similar pattern. As these examples suggest, digitized movements may be the wave of the future, but, like all waves, they seem to be ephemeral and liquid (Bauman 2000).

Allow me to clarify what I mean when I attribute liquidity to digitized movements. Compared to solids, liquids easily lose shape and dissipate. Social movements that recruit members mainly or exclusively through digital networks seem to share those properties with liquids. They do so for four reasons:

- First, joining such a network does not require long-term commitment, let alone risk-taking or sacrifice. Signing an online petition and contributing a dollar can constitute membership. This is the problem of what some analysts call slacktivism.

- Second, ours is an era in which people's interests, identities, and relationships change with relative ease, as sociologists of digital communications, families, sexualities, ethnicities, and religions never tire of pointing out. People have fluid social involvements, including involvements in social movements.

- Third, attention spans have shrunk since the cellphone revolution began around the year 2000. A Microsoft study found that the attention span of the average Canadian decreased by one-third between 2000 and 2013 and that cellphone use is especially widespread and intensive among young people, the main recruits of digitized social movements (Microsoft 2015). It seems we live in a communications environment that is hardly conducive to enduring involvements.

- Fourth, social movements that rely heavily or exclusively on digital networks to recruit members are liquid insofar as the application of counter-measures easily weakens them. Just as the Internet has been used to mobilize progressive activists, it has been used by non-progressives to successfully challenge perceived threats. Trump's 2016 presidential campaign provides only the most recent and startling example of how reactionary forces can use the Internet and social media to multiply their power and overcome the odds of failure (Brym et al. 2014; Brym et al. 2018; Harari 2018; Morozov 2011).

For these reasons, social movements organized mainly or exclusively through digital networks may be relatively short-lived and inconsequential. And so we arrive at the main challenge of social movements today, a challenge that commands the attention of the contributors to this volume: How can stable, effective social movement organizations be created when, as Marx and Engels put it, "all that is solid melts" (Marx and Engels 1848)?

About This Book
The following chapters turn on that question. Howard Ramos demonstrates the existence of a disjuncture between (1) the characteristics ascribed to social movements by leading researchers in the field and (2) the actual characteristics of many contemporary movements. He argues, in effect, that in the era of solidarity, critical outbursts of protest *followed* a period during which social forces gathered and built up a head of steam, while in the era of fluidity, such events typically explode *before* the crystallization of movement organization. The effective cooptation of movement tactics and technologies by authorities is also something new, as is the propagation of memes rather than programs and the direction of insurgents' anger at non-state institutions. Accordingly, rather than let established definitions blind us to what is new in the realm of social and political protest, Ramos makes a case for bridging the gap between established social movement definitions and facts on the ground. To that end, he argues that researchers need to develop a new definition based on inductive examination of the political actions that emerge during critical events occurring inside Bourdieusian socio-political fields.

Lesley Wood takes up Ramos's challenge in her analysis of protest activity in Canada and the United States in 2016–17. Specifically, she examines socio-political fields of action in both countries and situates them in their respective socio-political contexts. Wood finds that growing inequality along class, race, and other lines facilitated Trump's victory and his attack on democratic institutions. The right saw the moment as an opportunity, the left as a threat. They clashed frequently and sometimes violently, not as opposing monoliths but in various forms, with various organizations appealing to somewhat different population categories that pursued diverse but related goals and plans of action.

Catherine Corrigall-Brown shifts our attention from left-right clashes to the crystallization, actions, and staying power of left-wing protest movements (Indivisible groups) in the year after Trump's inauguration. She first compares five American cities in politically conservative areas with five in politically liberal areas. She finds that, while a similar number of Indivisible groups emerged in each type of political environment, they were much more active in liberal areas. Then comes a counterintuitive observation: Indivisible groups in conservative areas were more likely to be active after one year than were groups in liberal areas. How so?

To untie this knot, Corrigall-Brown compares conservative cities where the staying power of Indivisible groups varied. She finds that longevity was greater where groups engaged intensively in building coalitions with other organizations, tied political to non-political issues and events, and facilitated the engagement of new activists by reducing barriers to action. Corrigall-Brown thus offers a sort of recipe for increasing the staying power of movements in inhospitable political environments. The lesson for movements in Canada and other countries—and especially for people who are pessimistic about the prospects for left-wing movements in the current political climate—is that even in politically conservative areas, identifiable organizational mechanisms can be put in place to help movements endure.

In the 1990s, the adoption by the Tea Party of tactics, strategies, forms of protest, technologies, and organizational mechanisms formerly associated with left-wing movements surprised many observers and led to a flurry of research concerning movements on the right. Tina Fetner contributes significantly to this body of work by examining the different trajectories of the religious right in Canada and the United States. Wisely, she takes an historical and institutional approach to the problem.

Fetner points to two critical institutional junctures that led the religious right in the United States to grow into a force of enormous political influence while its Canadian counterpart became a political sideshow. In 1925, most evangelical churches in Canada coalesced to form the United Church of Canada while evangelical churches in the United States remained free to splinter. Coalescing favoured the middle ground. Splintering facilitated extremism. Then, in 1929, the Canadian government prohibited "statements of a controversial nature" in religious broadcasting and barred most advertising and solicitation of donations from audience members. The evangelical right in the United States grew rich and powerful on often outlandish controversy. Its Canadian counterpart became the impoverished, mild-mannered cousin to the north.

In the final chapter, Anna Slavina critically reviews the contributions of Ramos, Wood, Corrigall-Brown, and Fetner. She finds much of value in their work. She also demurs insofar as they do not explore cross-national variation in macro-level contexts that might help to account for variation in repertoires of contention, the durability of micro-level sites, relationships within fields, meso-level institutional relationships, and the other issues central to social movement studies. Slavina aims appropriately high, toward a synthesis of micro-, meso- and macro-levels of analysis. We await impatiently to see how that might be accomplished.

In sum, the authors of this volume have set themselves a difficult task—characterizing the present nature and future shape of mass dissent at a time when the social and political context is fluid and therefore poorly understood. They recognize the magnitude of the task, admit there is plenty of opportunity to slip and flounder in such a hazardous undertaking, yet offer valuable instruction on how we might yet learn to swim.

References

Andersen, Robert and Robert Brym. 2017. How terrorism affects attitudes towards democracy: Tunisia in 2015. *Canadian Review of Sociology* 54(4): 519–29.

Bauman, Zygmunt. 2000. *Liquid Modernity*. Cambridge, UK: Polity Press. https://bit.ly/2DjTQad.

Brym, Robert. 2019. *SOC+*, 4th ed. Toronto: Nelson.

Brym, Robert, Anna Slavina, Mina Todosijevic and David Cowan. 2018. Social movement horizontality in the Internet age? A comment on Castells in light of the Trump victory. *Canadian Review of Sociology* 55(4): 624–34.

Brym, Robert and Robert Andersen. 2016. Democracy, women's rights, and public opinion in Tunisia. *International Sociology* 31(2): 253–67.

Brym, Robert, Melissa Godbout, Andreas Hoffbauer, Gabriel Menard, and Tony Huiquan Zhang. 2014. Social media in the 2011 Egyptian uprising. *British Journal of Sociology* 65(2): 266–92.

Brym, Robert, Louise Birdsell Bauer, and Mitchell McIvor. 2013. Is industrial unrest reviving in Canada? Strike duration in the early 21st century. *Canadian Review of Sociology* 50(3): 222–33.

Castells, Manuel. 2012 [2015]. *Networks of Outrage and Hope: Social Movements in the Internet Age*, 2nd ed. Cambridge, UK: Polity Press.

Daragahi, Borzou. 2018. Belt-tightening demands put Tunisia's democracy at risk. *New York Times,* 3 May. https://nyti.ms/2Pdmfou.

Denton, F.T. 1976a. Table D1-7: Population of working age and either gainfully occupied or labour force, in non-agricultural and agricultural pursuits, census years, 1881 to 1971 (gainfully occupied 1881 to 1941, labour force 1951 to 1971). *The Labour Force*. Ottawa: Statistics Canada. http://www.statcan.gc.ca.ezcentennial.ocls.ca/pub/ll-516-x/sectiond/4057750-eng.htm#2.

Denton, F.T. 1976b. Table D260-265: Civilian persons with jobs in non-agricultural industries, by class of worker and sex, 1 June of each year, 1931 to 1981. *The Labour Force*. Ottawa: Statistics Canada. http://www.statcan.gc.ca.ezcentennial.ocls.ca/pub/11-516-x/sectiond/4057750-eng.htm#2.

Denton, F.T. 1976c. Table D236-259: Civilian employment in agriculture and non-agricultural industries, by class of worker and sex, annual averages, 1946 to 1971. *The Labour Force*. Ottawa: Statistics Canada. http://www.statcan.gc.ca.ezcentennial.ocls.ca/pub/ll-516-x/sectiond/4057750-eng.htm#2.

Diamond, Larry. 1996. Is the third wave over? *Journal of Democracy* 7(3): 20–37.

Dickens, Charles. 1859. *A Tale of Two Cities: A Story of the French Revolution*. https://bit.ly/2t2sdNR.

Freedom House. 2018. *Freedom in the World 2018: Democracy in Crisis*. https://bit.ly/2B4wj7t.

Froissart, Jean. c. 1365. Gaston Phébus et Jean de Grailli chargent les

Jacques et les parisiens qui tentent de prendre la forteresse du marché de Meaux où est retranchée la famille du Dauphin. (9 Juin 1358). *Chroniques, Flandre, Bruges.* https://bit.ly/2QiFn17.

Gastil, Raymond D. 1979. *Freedom in the World: Political Rights and Civil Liberties 1979.* Boston: G. K. Hall & Co. https://bit.ly/2DhCQ4k.

Harari, Yuval Noah. 2018. Why technology favors tyranny. *The Atlantic,* 31 August. https://bit.ly/2wwOh2m.

Huntington, Samuel. 1991. *The Third Wave: Democratization in the Late Twentieth Century.* Norman, OK: University of Oklahoma Press.

Marx, Karl. *The Poverty of Philosophy.* 1847 [1955]. https://bit.ly/2JxOoRh.

Marx, Karl and Friedrich Engels. 1848. Manifesto of the Communist Party. https://bit.ly/1hMQB8v.

Mayer, Gerald. 2004. Union membership trends in the United States. Washington DC: Congressional Research Service. https://bit.ly/2D3gaDT.

Meltz, N.M. 1976. Table E190-197: Number of strikes and lockouts, employers and workers involved and time loss, Canada, 1901–1975. *Wages and Working Conditions.* http://www5.statcan.gc.ca.ezcentennial. ocls.ca/access_acces/archive.action? l=eng&loc=E190_197-eng.csv.

Microsoft Canada. 2015. Attention spans. Toronto. https://bit.ly/2zCGm3B.

Morozov, Evgeny. 2011. *The Net Delusion: The Dark Side of Internet Freedom.* New York: Public Affairs.

Slavina, Anna, and Robert Brym. 2019. Demonstrating in the Internet age: A test of Castells' theory. *Social Movement Studies* 20(3).

Spengler, Oswald. 1918-22 [1927]. *The Decline of the West*, Charles Francis Atkinson, trans. New York: Alfred A. Knopf. https://bit.ly/2AJgXZd.

Statista. 2018. Canada: Union coverage rate in 2017, by province. https://bit.ly/2RDXf6R.

Statistics Canada. 2014. Table E175-177. Union membership in Canada, in total and as a percentage of non-agricultural paid workers and union members with international affiliation, 1911 to 1975. https://bit.ly/2qtEFTl.

Statistics Canada. 2018. Table 282-0088: Labour Force Survey estimates (LFS), employment by North American Industry Classification System (NAICS), seasonally adjusted and unadjusted monthly (persons x 1,000). http://www5.statcan.gc.ca/cansim/a26?id=2820088.

Tilly, Charles and Lesley J. Wood. 2004. [2013]. *Social Movements, 1768–2012*, 3rd ed. London: Routledge.

United States Department of Labor, Bureau of Labor Statistics. 2018. Union members—2017. https://bit.ly/2vA3T66.

CHAPTER TWO
Are Social Movements Still Relevant?

Howard Ramos

Increasingly, political action falls outside common academic definitions of "social movements." More and more political mobilization
tends to be event-centred, meme-focused, prefigurative (acting out
the future it seeks while ignoring existing institutions, norms, and
organizations), and discursive (focusing on meaning, words, and
narratives). Political action also increasingly transcends borders and
relies on social media and women leaders.

Social movement scholarship deals inadequately with these
characteristics because the repertoire of action associated with
mainstream social movement theory and research is bound to assumptions linked to the rise of states and democracy as well structural changes stemming from the Industrial Revolution. Much has
changed since then. Much contemporary contentious mobilization
takes place without reference to the state, and much of it is blurred
with mainstream politics. Moreover, in most recent high-profile cases of mobilization, movements emerge after critical events rather
than causing them, thus calling into question the mechanistic approach driven by dominant American social movement research
(e.g., McAdam et al. 2001). Because current parameterizations of
contentious politics pay insufficient attention to new and emerging
political phenomena, it is worth asking whether the social movement—as an academic concept and a political form—is still relevant
in the twenty-first century.

To engage this issue, I first identify how political-historical
contexts have influenced forms of contention and how conceptual-
izations of movements have varied accordingly. I then review key
definitions of social movements and examine how elements of those
definitions fit contemporary political action. Social movement societies, Indigenous resistance, anti-authoritarian mobilization, and
hashtag movements are discussed to identify common characteristics of contemporary mobilization and understand how the state and
democracy shape or fail to shape contemporary social movements.
I conclude by advocating an event- and field-centred approach to
studying movements as a means of identifying the concepts, actors,
and repertoires that define contemporary political struggles.

The importance of political-historical era in shaping forms of political contention

Modern social movements originated during the consolidation of states and democracy in the 1760s. A new merchant class was on the rise, and it fought for the creation of parliaments to institutionalize its grip on power (Mann 1986; Tilly and Wood 2013: 25). Social movements emerged as the modern state became the formal repository of power, and as a means of contesting its authority. The polity had become open enough to allow for contention but remained closed enough to prevent the overthrow of power holders, creating unprecedented space for political actors to challenge power while accepting the institutions that maintain it. In this context, social movements assumed unique properties and repertoires of political action that still mark some instances of contentious politics today (Tilly 1978; 2007; Tilly with Wood 2013). Social movements as a political form engaged in public demonstrations, occupations, and marches, hoisted banners displaying slogans and symbols, spanned numerous locales, and enjoyed broad and sustained participation. Academics still associate these characteristics with movements today.

As historical phenomena, movements evolved with the world around them (Crossley 2002; Diani 1992; Melucci 1980; Meyer and Tarrow 1998; Tilly and Wood 2013; Touraine, 1985). Dominant theories to account for them also evolved in relation to that changing world and reflect the political forms of the times. These observations imply that parameterization using old contexts and old concepts is bound to miss political forms emerging in new movements and new political-historical contexts that shape them. This circumstance leads me to ask whether social movements are a political form from a bygone era.

What are social movements?

Before answering this question, one must understand how social scientists define social movements. Diani (1992) and Crossley (2002) usefully analyze key definitions identifying core elements of the term.

Diani (1992) wrote in a period when the field was divided between North American and European scholars, with the former focusing on political structures, contexts, and rational actors and the latter on identity construction and postmaterialism. Diani drew attention to five leading scholars of collective behaviour, resource mobilization, political process, and new social movement theories. He argued that, across these perspectives and at their core, social movements are "networks of informal interactions between a plurality of individuals, groups and/or organizations, engaged in political or cultural conflicts, on the basis of shared collective identities" (Diani 1992: 1). He believed his definition distinguished the social movement as a political form from interest groups, political parties, protest events, and coalitions, yet was robust enough to include all elements needed to bridge competing perspectives that invoked the term for theoretical or analytic purposes.

Crossley (2002) wrote at the turn of the twenty-first century, when the field was less divided but the dominant political process approach seemed not to apply well to recent movements and actions. Globalization, neoliberalism, and the Seattle tactics were changing how politics was negotiated. Crossley examined how collective behaviour, political process, and network approaches explain social movements and introduced discussion of how a field approach developed by Bourdieu could be applied to the study of social movements. He aimed to introduce an actor-centred approach to research on contentious politics.

To explore the definitions that Diani and Crossley analyzed, as well as those deemed most relevant by Google Scholar, Table 1 summarizes the key characteristics of definitions of social movements in the popular academic literature. The Google Scholar search was conducted on 8 October 2018 using the search term: "social movements" definition. (For additional details, see http://perceptionsofchange.ca/socialmovementsstillrelevant.html.)

Table 1 identifies thirteen characteristics found across the definitions. For common definitions of social movements, a high degree of consensus was found on four terms: change, collective identity, conflict, and redistribution of rewards and power. A moderate level of consensus existed around five terms: action, beliefs/ideas/values, outsiders, social structures, and solidarity. Low consensus was found on four terms: networks, organization, purposiveness, and sustained action. Interestingly, despite the dominance of the American political process model, with its foundation in the resource mobilization tradition, the low-consensus terms are outliers rather than the norm for understanding social movements.

Can contemporary forms of contention be adequately defined by these points and levels of consensus? If not, we must reconceptualize the form political contention takes and ask whether the label of social movement is appropriate. Most definitions of social movements distinguish movements from the contexts in which they emerge, positioning them as political actors outside the mainstream that take radical, public, protest-oriented actions. The next section explores the importance of political-historical context by examining links between movements, on the one hand, and protest and democratic nation-states, on the other. It sets out to determine the degree to which links discovered in the past are present today.

Table 2.1. Characteristics of definitions of social movements

Consensus	Characteristics
High	Change; collective identity; conflict; redistribution of rewards and power
Medium	Actions/behaviour; beliefs/ideas/values; outsiders; social structure; solidarity
Low	Networks; organization; purpose; sustained action

Contradictions in declining democracy yet continuing protest

The question of whether social movements are still relevant stems from a contradiction observed in contemporary politics. Around the world we see increasing threats to democracy but an apparent rise in protest. This shift is important given that social movements have tended to be linked to democratic states or the rise of democratic institutions (Tilly 1978; Tilly and Wood 2013). Examining the state of democracy across contemporary societies leads to the conclusion that its future is uncertain. Is the current context conducive to social movements or is it spawning new forms of contention?

Much research concludes that democracy is weakening. For instance, Freedom House declared that democracy is in "crisis," with almost two-thirds of states losing democratic freedoms over the last twelve years (Abramowitz 2018). The same conclusion was reached by the Cato Institute and affiliated think tanks by examining personal, economic, and human freedom in 159 countries from 2008 to 2015 (Vasquez and Porcnik 2017). More than half the regions in the world are experiencing a decline in freedom and, on average, declines are greater than improvements. Notably, declines are seen in many parts of Europe and North America, known for being more open and established democracies, as well as in Latin American. *The Economist*'s global democracy index fell between 2016 and 2017 due to a decline in 89 countries, thus leading to the conclusion that democracy is under attack (The Economist Intelligence Unit 2017).

Change over time in the 2018 Edelman Global Trust Index indicates "a world of distrust," with most people in most countries no longer trusting institutions (Edelman 2018). Many people worry that lack of institutional trust gives rise to neo-fascism (Giroux 2016; Kellner 2016). Electoral victories of leaders in the Philippines, Hungary, Turkey, Brazil, and the United States who claim to speak for "the people" while working to curb freedom of expression, undermine political institutions, and fan ethnic or racial tensions are cases in point. Such trends, although much weaker, are apparent in Canada too, as evidenced by the election of "populist" premiers in Ontario and Quebec in 2018.

Since 2006, global protest has increased across a wide range of issues including economic justice and austerity, failure of political representation, rights, and global justice, and this is especially the case in high-income countries (Ortiz et al. 2013). Almost 20 percent of Americans said they had participated in a protest or rally since 2016 (Sampathkumar 2018). However, Goldstone (2004) warns that much of that mobilization occurs within a broader field of political actions, and numbers may be inflated because of cross-fertilization between forms of political action. Biggs (2015) shows this to be the case in the UK, where protest numbers are inflated by strikes and other political actions being reported as protests in many datasets. When that is taken into account, the number of people participating in protests actually declines. In other words, there is more reporting of protest but fewer people protesting.

This pattern can be seen in Canada through Cycles 17, 22, and 27 of the General Social Survey, which measure several types of political practice. Table 2.2 shows mixed and, for the most part, undramatic trends. Voting in federal elections increased slightly from 2003 to 2013, but the trend has been downward since 1958 (Brym, Roberts, and Strohschein 2019: 375). Between 2003 and 2013, the percentage of people saying they signed a petition barely changed, while the percentage of people boycotting or choosing products for ethical or political reasons increased only a little. The percentage of people saying they attended public meetings fell substantially, and there was a small drop in the percentage of people saying they engaged in demonstrations. In the latter case, one of the biggest drops occurred among those who were 18 to 24 years old at the time of the survey. Among 18-to-24-year-olds, a 2.5 percentage point drop occurred during the period under consideration (from 12.0 percent to 9.5 percent), slightly more than the 1.5 percentage point drop for the entire population. It appears that fewer Canadians are protesting, especially younger Canadians.

What do these trends mean for social movements?

Table 2.2. Canadian political practices, 2003–13

	2003	2008	2013
Voted in federal election	70.6	73.3	73.0
Searching for political information	25.7	28.8	38.9
Signing a petition	28.4	24.7	27.5
Boycotting or choosing a product for ethical reasons	20.7	26.9	23.0
Attending a public meeting	22.1	18.5	15.3
Participating in a demonstration	6.1	3.9	4.6

Source: General Social Survey, Cycles 17, 22, and 27 (Social Identity), Statistics Canada-PUMF. Compiled by Rachel McLay, Dalhousie University.

What fits the concept of social movement?

If we examine contemporary contentious politics and the phenomena labelled social movements, we find numerous political actions that do not fit existing definitions of "social movement." For example, social movements are increasingly hard to distinguish from other forms of political action, and their language and tactics are increasingly coopted by dominant power holders, nativists, and professional organizations (Meyer 2015; Meyer and Tarrow 1998). When such cooptation occurs, the concept of social movement becomes overstretched and hollowed out. Another example of discontinuity between definition and reality is Indigenous mobilization that resists colonization and, in doing so, pursues self-determination, often in a manner that is prefigurative (Wilkes 2015). When this occurs, the acceptance of the state as the vessel of power is questioned, and the alternative consists of acts of resistance that are not merely protest but actions in pursuit of a new form of power. Still other examples can be seen in the rise of anti-authoritarian movements like the Arab Spring and hashtag movements like Occupy and #MeToo, which in some cases challenge the state outright and in others have no predefined purpose, identity, or solidarity and which lack clearly defined goals and plans of engagement with power structures. In these cases, we witness contentious action, but it is unclear whether we are witnessing social movements as conventionally understood. Most recent political movements tend to be defined by events, memes, and the technology that facilitates them, requiring that we inspect them through a non-parameterized analytic lens to see what, if anything, is different about their struggle for power, their repertoire of action, and their form of politics.

Social movement societies: Make America Great Again
More than two decades ago, David Meyer and Sidney Tarrow (1998) argued that advanced democracies were becoming "social movement societies." They held that mobilization had changed from risky, contentious, and extra-state action in the 1960s to predictable and accommodating action that was partly incorporated into the state by the 1990s. In Canada, their argument certainly holds weight because of the longstanding reliance of many advocacy organizations on government funding and the consequent blurring of state and movement (Ramos and Rodgers 2015). This means that although movement organizations have been critical of authority, many cannot claim independence of the state. Thus, some English-Canadian women's social movement organizations were unable to sustain themselves in the face of government funding cuts (Rodgers and Knight 2011). In revisiting the social movement society thesis, Meyer (2015) encouraged researchers to focus on how it is associated with the cooptation of social movement tactics and language by nativists, which is abetted by new technologies (including social media and other Internet-based platforms) and the silos of communication and community they create.

All these trends are linked to the rise of Donald Trump. He repeatedly used the term "movement" to describe his actions and rally the support of his base, and some social movement scholars have used the term to describe his mobilization and that of the Tea Party which preceded it (Rohlinger and Bunnage 2017; Roth, B. 2018; Roth, S. 2018). Trump also famously claimed to be running as an outsider and, in fact, worked outside the Republican organization. His presidency has used similar tactics and positioning (Gunn 2017).

Each of the core elements that define a social movement applies to Trump's "Make America Great Again" (MAGA) campaign and what he calls a movement. Consider the high-consensus elements in Table 2.1. Trump pursued change, created or amplified a collective identity, positioned himself in conflict with mainstream politics, and did so in the name of redistributing power and status. These initiatives are all drivers of his MAGA meme. If we focus on the elements of social movements concerning which there is a medium level of consensus, we see that Trump does not promote actions traditionally linked to social movements. However, he uses beliefs and attitudes to build his movement; he (ironically) positions himself and his supporters as outsiders, although he and many of them have held power; he does not overtly challenge the social structure of society or the state, although he challenges political parties and leaders and, by doing so, has weakened the state; and he has created solidarity in his base but deep divisions in American society. Among the low-consensus aspects of what researchers consider a social movement, we find that Trump's mobilization taps networks and analytics used to micro-target people who would otherwise be unconnected; he has relied on organization, largely members of his family and those in his business network; he set out with a clear agenda—to gain power and maintain it; and he has sustained his actions and that of his base as he continues to mobilize people. This case illustrates a key problem with the contemporary definition of "social movement": it is so broad it can be applied to movements that many if not most researchers in the field would not consider social movements.

The case of MAGA illustrates other issues in contemporary social movement scholarship. Much of Trump's mobilization was fueled by social media, Twitter and Facebook in particular (Gunn 2017: 53), and it mined data on followers (Brym et al. 2018; Pybus 2019). This method of mobilization gave his movement the appearance of having a multi-directional, non-hierarchical (or "rhizomatic") pattern of diffusion and structure that was fueled by memes or key slogans (Castells 2015). These features are increasingly common in contentious political action, but they may or may not align with what researchers consider social movements.

Indigenous movements: Idle No More
Cooptation of movement language and tactics, and the blurring of movements with other political forms, are trends that have been observed for at least 20 years. Another form of mobilization that challenges the concept of social movement is Indigenous resistance. This is especially the case in Canada, where the legal rights of Indigenous peoples are recognized in the constitution and as the country engages in a quest for "reconciliation'" that is meant to come to terms with its history of colonization (Ramos 2008; 2006; Wilkes et al. 2017). Both trends make Indigenous mobilization different than other movements in Canada.

In a critical review of the legacy of her work on Indigenous mobilization, Rima Wilkes (2015) questions whether it is the same as protest, and, in turn, whether the analytical tools of social movement research can be used to understand Indigenous political action. She argues that treating Indigenous movements like other social movements fails to recognize the territorial and colonial elements associated with Indigenous mobilization and that the state has been imposed on original inhabitants who do not necessarily recognize its legitimacy or the legitimacy of the institutions it creates (Alfred, 1999). Most social movements accept the state as the site of ultimate authority, but traditional Indigenous movements largely resist that view. Ignoring this difference can lead to erroneous interpretations of events and actions.

With respect to the four high-consensus elements of the academic definition of social movements, just one seems to apply to Idle No More: change. Those acting in the name of the hashtag were seeking to stop the federal government from acting without consulting Indigenous peoples. Yet the demands of the movement were never fully articulated; despite having clear initiators it did not have obvious leaders. The movement had an ambiguous collective identity, with strong generational and identity divisions among Indigenous communities. It tended to avoid outright conflict. Although some actors suggested more radical tactics, few took place; unlike similar national protests in the 1990s, there was little violence or threat of it. The movement also did not seek redistribution of power or rewards, but was rather defensive in nature and, above all, educational, encouraging Indigenous peoples to return to their traditional teachings and relationship to the environment.

Examining the elements of medium consensus, we find that two fit the movement—actions/behaviour and beliefs/ideas/values. The movement was event- and action-based, with round dances and social media posts as its main activities. The movement was a call for action based on traditional beliefs and values. It was not a movement that positioned itself as an outsider and did not engage in directly changing social structures or building solidarity. It was a movement based on individuals responding to calls to action.

None of the elements of low consensus fit Idle No More. Despite Wood's (2015) claim that the movement relied on established networks, it did not look like past Indigenous mobilization and introduced a new generation of activists. It was not formally organized. Its purpose was originally to mobilize against certain legislation but it moved beyond that when the government tried to negotiate with its presumed leaders, and the action was not sustained. As quickly as the movement emerged, it disappeared.

As with MAGA, Idle No More was defined by a meme, which may have offered the appearance of a rhizomatic structure, and it was heavily dependent on social media for communication and the spread of information. It was prefigurative in its actions. Rather than making demands on the state, it was a call to action to show how the state did not align with Indigenous values. It was a call for people to return to their traditional teachings and resist colonization by practicing traditional values. As with other recent movements and recent contentious politics, women were key political actors in initiating the movement.

Anti-authoritarian movements: the Arab Spring

As noted earlier, social movements have tended to be linked to democratic states or those seeking to liberalize. One of the key criticisms of American social movement theory has been that it does not work well in explaining movements in authoritarian states or the developing world (McAdam et al. 2001). With the demonstrations of the so-called "Arab Spring," several social movement scholars have used social movement and network theory to try to understand the rapid mobilization and diffusion of the mobilization from Tunisia, to Egypt, to the rest of the region, and subsequently the rest of the world (e.g., Brym et al. 2014; Castells 2012; Tufecki 2017; Tufecki and Wilson 2012). The movement began after a young street vendor set himself on fire in 2010 to "protest against the humiliation of repeated confiscation of his fruit and vegetable stand by the local police after he refused to pay a bribe" (Castells 2012: 22). His act sparked demonstrations by other youths after being posted on the Internet through social media. The protests spread across the country, resulting in more videos of protests and police violence taken with smartphones and transmitted through new communications platforms, such as Twitter. It gave youth and other contentious political actors an unfiltered means of communication, linking people in unprecedented ways (Tufecki 2017). The protesters demanded democracy and they toppled regimes across the region. It also inspired actions in other countries, such as the Maple Spring in Quebec and Occupy Wall Street.

Castells (2012) argues that rhizomatic structures and social media generated the action and led to its widespread diffusion not only across the Middle East but to other movements around the world. Brym et al. (2014) highlight the importance of established organizations that responded to events and helped support protesters and amplify their efforts. Tufecki (2017) places less emphasis on existing structures and instead notes that the movement's early success was based on its use of new media platforms, which authorities did not control, in a fluid political context. Tufecki, a participant in several Arab Spring events, highlights the fragility of such movements. She notes that new media allowed rapid mobilization, but networks, organization, and identity were largely built in reaction to the events and memes rather than sparking them. Because of this event-centredness, each part of the movement was open to repression once power holders developed counter-measures and tactics. The technology and networks that led to mobilization were eventually used to repress the movement and have increasingly been used by populist movements and those seeking to destabilize democratic institutions.

When this type of mobilization is examined in light of the elements of social movements on which strong consensus exists, we see clear demands for change and liberalization among Arab Spring movement actors, an ambiguous collective identity formed in the course of action, a challenge to authority and occupation of space, and a demand for redistribution of power. With respect to elements on which there exists medium consensus, the movement was action-based, revolving around critical events and occupations, and it was solidly built around collective beliefs. However, it is unclear how or if actors were positioned as outsiders; they demanded change in social structures, but it is uncertain whether solidarity existed until after mobilization. Tufecki (2013; 2017) notes that many actors were constructing their microcelebrity as much as they were posting about the movement. As a result, identity and solidarity were constructed after rather than before events. The same can be said with respect to low consensus elements of social movements, such as networks, which in many cases were loose and formed through social media interactions, and organization, which emerged from events rather than driving their occurrence. In many locations the movement was born out of individuals acting alone out of frustration. Action was sustained for the short term, but like other recent movements it dissipated almost as quickly as it emerged.

Like other recent political forms of contention, many of the core elements of classic social movement definitions occurred after critical events rather than being the drivers of events. This means that much recent mobilization is event-centred. Such sequencing is more in line with early collective behaviour approaches rather than the mechanism-focused approach of political process theory that dominates American research (e.g., McAdam et al. 2001).

Hashtag movements: Occupy, #BlackLivesMatter, and #MeToo
Many of the features observed in the Arab Spring's mobilization are also evident in other movements that have emerged since. In part, that is because the Arab Spring inspired successor movements (Castells 2012). Perhaps its biggest influence was on Occupy Wall Street, hereafter Occupy, which was also inspired by protests around the

world against inequities associated with the 2008–09 global economic crisis (Gitlin 2013). Occupy took off after Vancouver-based Adbusters issued a call to occupy Wall Street in September 2011. In many ways, the movement's name is the result of the meme generated by the group. Occupy did not have formal leaders or formalized demands. It was loosely organized, and it developed a unique repertoire of actions, including the human microphone. It also generated its own memes, such as "We are the 99%" which brought discussion of income inequality to the forefront of public discussion (Gitlin 2013; Calhoun 2013). The movement's memes and style of mobilization spread to over 80 countries and more than 600 cities.

Castells (2012) described how Occupy was characterized by the occupation of space and loose, rhizomatic networks. It also had many of the features of the global justice movement, sharing a lineage with the Seattle tactics (della Porta 2008). Yet it was different in several ways. In particular, it was more a moment than a movement (Gitlin 2013). It began with a large and diffuse support base consisting of unnetworked people, which led to tensions between core movement actors and those who responded with less direct action.

Overall, the standard elements used to define a social movement do not fare well in describing Occupy. Among the four high-consensus elements of a social movement, only two are met by the movement: the hope for change and an attempt to achieve redistribution of resources. In terms of the medium consensus elements, Occupy was action-based and event-centred. However, it did not enunciate a clear consensus on beliefs or values and it is unclear how actors were positioned. It focused on prefigurative performance of alternative values, but it is unclear whether widespread solidarity emerged in the movement. The low consensus elements do not fare well: it is uncertain whether networks were fully utilized; new networks emerged; and people simply responded to a meme. Organization emerged *in situ*, but there was little coordination across sites or even within Occupy encampments. The purpose of the movement was to fight economic inequality, but Occupy lacked leaders and clear demands, and the movement was sustained for only a few months before largely disappearing.

Space does not permit detailed analysis of other movements, such as Black Lives Matter or #MeToo. However, Table 2.3 explores how they compare to movements discussed here by highlighting emergent features of contemporary movements and the forms their politics takes. In brief, Table 2.3 demonstrates that many features of what researchers refer to as social movements do not apply to

Table 2.3. Characteristics of recent movements

	Characteristics of movement	MAGA	#IdleNoMore	Arab Spring	Occupy	#BlackLives-Matter	#MeToo
Core social movement concepts	Action/behavior	?	X	X	X	X	X
	Beliefs/ideas/values	X	X	X	X	X	X
	Challenge/conflict	X		X			
	Change	X	X	X	X	X	X
	Collective (identity)	X		?	X	X	
	Networks	X		?	?		
	Organized	?		?			
	Outsider	X		?		X	?
	Purposive	?	?	?			
	Redistribution of rewards/power	X		X	X		
	Social structure	?		X			
	Solidarity	X		?			
	Sustained	X					
Contemporary movement characteristics	Event-centred		X	X	X	X	X
	Meme	X	X	X	X	X	X
	Rhizomatic	?	?	?	?	?	?
	Prefigurative		X	X	X	X	X
	Redefinition of discourse	X	X	X	X	X	X
	Social media use	X	X	X	X	X	X
	Transnational			X	X	X	X
	Women		X			X	X

Note: An "x" signifies that the element was present in the movement. A "?" signifies it is unclear whether the element was present in the movement. An empty cell signifies that the element was not present in the movement.

contemporary movements. Common across recent movements are event-centredness, or politics driven by critical events; the importance of memes; the use of social media and new technology; and having a primary effect on public discourse, not the state.

What will the Fourth Industrial Revolution mean for social movements?

Recent movements have pushed the limits of how researchers parameterize "social movements." In part this may be the result of the changing political-historical context. Recall that social movements as a political form emerged with the Industrial Revolution, a profound technological shift. As the world is currently entering a "Fourth Industrial Revolution" (Schwab 2016) characterized by the power of information, new technology, robotics, algorithms, and artificial intelligence, one must again ask how these changes will affect political forms and power contests.

Early signs indicate that new technology is giving the upper hand to authoritarian leaders. It has been coopted to mobilize populist forces and it has become a tool for repressive states to clamp down on its citizens. China's use of facial recognition software is an example of the latter. The technology has been deployed mainly to supress Tibetans, Uyghurs, and other minorities or dissidents. Bots that troll political supporters have been used in conjunction with the technology. Artificial intelligence was key to Russian interference in the 2016 American election as well electoral races throughout Europe. Added to the mix is the role of large information companies such as Amazon, Google, Facebook, and Apple. Most of the world's information passes through one of the four, and their teams and algorithms control the flow of what is said, seen, and heard.

To date, the information power of the Fourth Industrial Revolution is largely unregulated. If states are late reining it in, the technology and power that comes with it could soon outpace states in meeting the needs of people and in turn challenge them for power. In many respects this is already beginning to happen and may usher in a new political-historical era. Yet social movement researchers and social scientists still theorize and conceptualize power using old parameterizations. What these new developments will mean for social movements and forms of political resistance are unclear. What is clear is that we need new concepts to understand the shifting political-historical context and emerging forms of politics. How do we derive them?

An event-centred, field approach to twenty-first century contentious politics

We cannot predict what political resistance will look like in the rest of the twenty-first century. What is clear is that protest still matters, for now, and most contemporary mobilization is event-centred. If this is the case it is fruitful to adopt an "eventful" approach to understanding political contention (della Porta 2008; Sewell 1996). Such an approach examines historical context as a matter of ebbs and flows, recognizing that some events have a bigger impact on societies and their political economy than do others, with rare events being transformational, changing institutions and their practices and disrupting taken-for-granted assumptions and power relations (Sewell 2005; 1996; Staggenborg 1993; Wood et al. 2017). As the form of politics changes, and as the containers of power (states) are challenged by changing political-historical forces, focusing on events might be the appropriate way to navigate these changes.

An event-centred approach examines assemblages of concepts, actors, actions, and social relations that emerge as fields of power and politics around events. It takes on a non-parameterized mode of investigation; such an inductive approach allows researchers to identify the correlations among political actions (Goldstone 2004) and in doing so can help identify new actions, tactics, and actors. The approach also avoids trends that are overlooked by the prescriptive and parameterized approaches that have come to dominate mainstream social movement research. To this end, we would be well advised to adopt a Bourdieusian approach to the study of contentious politics.

Bourdieu's non-parameterized theory and his use of correspondence analysis illustrate how fields of capital are created and overlap. He shows how differences across commonly held parameterizations of social dimensions come apart when they are no longer assumed *a priori* and are instead seen as distributions of actions and practices without pre-definition or expectation. If social movements researchers follow suit, we will be able to examine power as it emerges in struggles around critical events that trigger fields (Sewell 2005). Once fields are identified, researchers can then analyze the actors, actions, and power-holders that interact and contest power within it (Fligstein and McAdam 2011; 2012).

The utility of a field approach inheres in its ability to deal with fuzziness across boundaries and concepts (Crossley 2002). It is not deterministic and is thus useful for examining movement practices and forms (Haluza-DeLay 2008). It is useful for analyzing newly emerging contexts. An event-centred, field approach considers assemblages of relations or concepts that correspond to a triggering event which sparks a field or, as seen in Table 2.3, how actions and practices missed by existing concepts fit into the repertoire of power struggles around recent movements. Rather than sticking to our old concepts and parameterizations, we need to move forward by mapping what is done in practice, which in turn can be used to identify the forces that will structure future contentious politics. Only such an approach can fully answer the question of whether social movements are still relevant.

References

Abramowitz, Michael J. 2018. Democracy in crisis. *Freedom House in the World 2018.* https://freedomhouse.org/sites/default/files/FH_FITW_Report_2018_Final_SinglePage.pdf.

Alfred, Taiaiake. 1999. *Peace, Power, Righteousness: An Indigenous Manifesto.* Toronto: Oxford University Press.

Biggs, Michael. 2015. Has protest increased since the 1970s? How a survey question can construct a spurious trend. *British Journal of Sociology* 66(1): 141–62.

Brym, Robert, Melissa Godbout, Andreas Hoffbauer, Gabe Menard, and Tony Huiquan Zhang. 2014. Social media in the 2011 Egyptian uprising. *British Journal of Sociology* 65(2): 266–92.

Brym, Robert, Anna Slavina, Mina Todosijevic, and David Cowan. 2018. Social movement horizontality in the Internet age? A comment on Castells in light of the Trump victory. *Canadian Review of Sociology* 55(4): 624–34

Brym, Robert, Lance W. Roberts, and Lisa Strohschein. 2019. *Sociology: Compass for a New Social World*, 6th ed. Toronto: Nelson.

Calhoun, Craig. 2013. Occupy Wall Street in perspective. *British Journal of Sociology* 64(1): 26–38.

Castells, Manuel. 2015. *Networks of Outrage and Hope: Social Movements in the Internet Age.* New York: Wiley.

Caven, Febna. 2013. Being idle no more: The women behind the movement. *Cultural Survival Quarterly* 37(1): 6–7.

Crossley, Nick. 2002. *Making Sense of Social Movements.* London: McGraw-Hill Education.

Crossley, Nick. 2003. From reproduction to transformation: Social movement fields and the radical habitus. *Theory, Culture, and Society* 20(6): 43–68.

della Porta, Donatella. 2008. Eventful protest, global conflicts. *Distinktion: Scandinavian Journal of Social Theory* 9(2): 27–56.

della Porta, Donatella and Sidney Tarrow. 2005. Transnational processes and social activism: An introduction. Pp. 1–20 in *Transnational Protest and Global Activism*, D. della Porta and S. Tarrow, eds. Lanham, MD: Rowman & Littlefield Publishers, Inc.

della Porta, Donatella, Massimiliano Andretta, Lorenzo Mosca, and Herbert Reiter. 2006. *Globalization from Below: Transnational Activists and Protest Networks.* Minneapolis, MN: University of Minnesota Press.

Diani, Mario. 1992. The concept of social movement. *The Sociological Review* 40(1): 1–25.

Edelman 2018. Global report. *2018 Edelman Trust Barometer.* https://www.edelman.com/sites/g/files/aatuss191/files/2018-10/2018_Edelman_Trust_Barometer_Global_Report_FEB.pdf.

Fligstein, Niel and Doug McAdam. 2012. *A Theory of Fields.* New York: Oxford University Press.

Fligstein, Niel and Doug McAdam. 2011. Toward a general theory of strategic action fields. *Sociological Theory* 29(1): 1–26.

Gitlin, Todd. 2013. Occupy's predicament: The moment and the prospects for the movement. *British Journal of Sociology* 64: 3–25.

Giroux, Henry A. 2016. Donald Trump and neo-fascism in America. *Arena Magazine* 140: 31.

Goldstone, Jack A. 2004. More social movements or fewer? Beyond political opportunity structures to relational fields. *Theory and Society* 33(3): 333–65.

Gunn, Enli. 2017. Twitter as arena for the authentic outsider: Exploring the social media campaigns of Trump and Clinton in the 2016 US presidential election. *European Journal of Communication* 32(1): 50–61.

Haluza DeLay, Randolph. 2008. A theory of practice for social movements: Environmentalism and ecological habitus. *Mobilization* 13(2): 205–18.

Inman, Derek, Stefean Smis, and Dorothée Cambou. 2013. We will remain idle no more: The shortcomings of Canada's duty to consult Indigenous peoples. *Goettingen Journal of. International Law* 5: 251.

Kellner, Douglas. 2016. The resurrection of Richard Nixon and American neo-fascism. Pp. 41–3 in *American Nightmare*. Rotterdam: SensePublishers.

Mann, Michael. 1986. *The Sources of Social Power: The Rise of Classes and Nation-States, 1760–1914,* vol. 2. Cambridge, UK: Cambridge University Press.

McAdam, Doug, Sidney G. Tarrow, and Charles Tilly. 2001. *Dynamics of Contention*. Cambridge, UK: Cambridge University Press.

McMillan, L. Jane, Janelle Young, and Molly Peters. 2013. Commentary: The "idle no more" movement in Eastern Canada. *Canadian Journal of Law and Society/La Revue Canadienne Droit et Société* 28(3): 429–31.

Melucci, Alberto. 1980. The new social movements: A theoretical approach. *Information (International Social Science Council)* 19(2): 199–226.

Meyer, David S. 2015. Reconsidering the social movement society in the new century. Pp. 21–43 in *Protest and Politics: The Promise of Social Movement Societies*, H. Ramos and K. Rodgers, eds. Vancouver: UBC Press.

Meyer, David S. and Sidney Tarrow. 1998. A movement society: Contentious politics for a new century. Pp 1–28 in *The Social Movement Society: Contentious Politics for a New Century*. Lanham, MD: Rowman & Littlefield Publishers, Inc.

Ortiz, Isabel, Sara Burke, Mohamed Berrada and Heran Cortés. 2013. World protests 2006–2013. New York: Initiative for Policy Dialogue and Friedrich-Ebert-Stiftung. http://policydialogue.org/files/publications/papers/World_Protests_2006-2013-Complete_and_Final_4282014.pdf.

Pybus, Jennifer. 2019. Trump, the first Facebook president: Why politicians need our data too. Pp. 227–40 in *Trump's Media War*. New York: Palgrave Macmillan, Cham.

Ramos, Howard. 2006. What causes Canadian Aboriginal protest? Examining resources, opportunities and identity, 1951–2000. *Canadian Journal of Sociology* 31(2): 211–34.

Ramos, Howard. 2008. Opportunity for whom? Political opportunity and critical events in Canadian Aboriginal mobilization, 1951–2000. *Social Forces* 87(2): 795–824.

Ramos, Howard, and Kathleen Rodgers, eds. 2015. *Protest and Politics: The Promise of Social Movement Societies.* Vancouver: UBC Press.

Rodgers, Kathleen and Melanie Knight. 2011. "You just felt the collective wind being knocked out of us": The deinstitutionalization of feminism and the survival of women's organizing in Canada. *Women's Studies International Forum* 34: 570–81.

Rohlinger, Deana A. and Leslie Bunnage. 2017. "Did the Tea Party movement fuel the Trump-train? The role of social media in activist persistence and political change in the 21st century. *Social Media+Society* 3(2): 1–11. https://doi.org/10.1177/2056305117706786.

Roth, Benita. 2018. Learning from the Tea Party: The US indivisible movement as countermovement in the era of Trump. *Sociological Research Online* 23(2): 539–46.

Roth, Silke. 2018. Contemporary counter-movements in the age of Brexit and Trump. *Sociological Research Online* 23(2): 496–506. https://doi.org/10.1177/1360780418768828.

Schwab, Klaus. 2016. The Fourth Industrial Revolution: What it means, how to respond. World Economic Forum. https://www.weforum.org/agenda/2016/01/the-fourth-industrial-revolution-what-it-means-and-how-to-respond/.

Sewell, William H., Jr. 1996. Three temporalities: Toward an eventful sociology. Pp. 245–80 in *The Historic Turn in the Human Sciences*, Terrence McDonald, ed. Ann Arbor, MI: University of Michigan Press.

Sewell, William H., Jr. 2005. *Logics of History: Social Theory and Social Transformation.* Chicago: University of Chicago Press.

Staggenborg, Suzanne. 1993. Critical events and the mobilization of the pro-choice movement. *Research in Political Sociology* 6(1): 319–45.

Tilly, Charles. 1978. *From Mobilization to Revolution.* Reading, MA: Addison-Wesley.

Tilly, Charles and Lesley J. Wood. 2013. *Social Movements, 1768–2012*, 3rd ed. Boulder, CO: Paradigm.

Touraine, Alain. 1985. An introduction to the study of social movements. *Social Research* 52(4): 749–87.

Tufekci, Zeynep. 2017. *Twitter and tear gas: The power and fragility of networked protest.* New Haven, CT: Yale University Press.

Tufekci, Zeynep and Christopher Wilson. 2012. Social media and the decision to participate in political protest: Observations from Tahrir Square. *Journal of Communication* 62(2): 363–79.

Vásquez, Ian and Tanja Porcnik. 2017. The human freedom index, 2017. https://object.cato.org/sites/cato.org/files/human-freedom-index-files/2017-human-freedom-index-2.pdf.

Wilkes, Rima. 2015. Indigenous resistance in comparative perspective: An overview with an autobiographical research critique." Pp. 111–128 in *"More Will Sing Their Way to Freedom": Indigenous Resistance and Resurgence*, Elaine Coburn, ed. Halifax, NS: Fernwood Press.

Wilkes, Rima, Aaron Duong, Linc Kesler, and Howard Ramos. 2017. Canadian university acknowledgment and recognition of Indigenous lands, treaties, and peoples. *Canadian Review of Sociology* 54(1): 89–120.

Wood, Lesley J. 2014. *Crisis and Control: The Militarization of Protest Policing*. Toronto: Between the Lines

Wood, Lesley J. 2015. "Idle No More, Facebook and Diffusion." *Social Movement Studies* 14(5): 615–21.

Wood, Leslie J., S. Staggenborg, G. J. Stalker, G. J., and R. Kutz-Flamenbaum. 2017. Eventful events: Local outcomes of G20 summit protests in Pittsburgh and Toronto. *Social Movement Studies* 16(5): 1–15.

Wotherspoon, Terry and John Hansen. 2013. The "Idle No More" movement: Paradoxes of First Nations inclusion in the Canadian context. *Social Inclusion* 1(1): 21–36.

CHAPTER THREE

Antifa and Alt-Right: Movement/Counter-movement Dynamics in the Post-Trump Era

Lesley J. Wood

What is the future of social movements in Canada? These days, a lot of fast theorizing is taking place, with competing stories that sound a bit like the old tale of the blind men describing an elephant. One fellow argues that we are amidst a massive wave of protest. He notes that the Women's March was the largest single day of mobilization in United States history, with protests in hundreds of cities and towns. In the United States, frequent, large, and fast mobilizations recur around a range of electoral issues, including immigration, the Trump election, and gun violence. A second blind man argues that politics has been replaced by brawling. From this point of view, the partisan nature of politics has made social movements no longer a channel for politics but simply a battle between right and left. A third person notes that social movements are now primarily online. He mentions #MeToo and the alt-right, suggesting that looking at street protests misses the real site of the action (Brym et al. 2017, Castells 2012, Gerbaudo 2012, Tufekci 2017). A fourth bystander suggests that the left has collapsed and that we have ceded the streets to right-wing movements.

While there is some truth to all these claims, we clearly need to be more systematic in our analysis of movements in the current moment if we want to get a sense of what the future of social movements in Canada and the United States might be. To that end, I will describe the current moment in protest activity in both countries. I find that Trump triggered a wave of both left and especially right-wing protest, increasing protester/counter-protester interactions. The scale and shape of these interactions are shaped by durable inequalities and declining democracy, fragmented social networks, and divided strategies of contention.

Looking back, gazing ahead

In 2003, Charles Tilly argued that the future of social movements was uncertain. He proposed four possibilities:

1. *Internationalization.* In this scenario, social movements shift to international targets and organize internationally. This seemed to be the case in 2003, with the increasing importance of international financial institutions and international nongovernmental organizations (NGOs) as protest targets. It was a period of globalized anti-war, human rights, and global justice movements.
2. *Democratic decline.* Tilly argued that, because of weakening democracy in major democracies, a second possibility is "increasing differentiation of social movement practices across those surviving enclaves, as communication and coordination among the world's social movement activists [diminish] and as local or regional activists [adapt] to their particular conditions."
3. *Professionalization.* The third potential trajectory Tilly noted was professionalization, involving a shift from innovative local and regional grassroots action to institutionalized and isomorphic national and international non-profit and advocacy organizations.
4. *Triumph.* Finally, Tilly surmised we might reach victory or "people power." For this to occur, social movements would have to build and gain power, resulting in democratization and decentralization (Tilly and Wood 2013: 154–59).

Since Tilly's observations, researchers have analyzed evidence of internationalization and professionalization of some movements; many movements operate without a grassroots base and therefore without accountable relationships to such a base (Smith et al. 2017, Tarrow 2004). However, it is the decline of democracy and the relationship of the decline to contention that interests me most. It is the scenario least developed in Tilly's list, and the one that, I think, most urgently requires unpacking.

Throughout his work, Tilly keeps the relationship between regimes of powerholders and repertoires of contention central. He tracks changes in contention by examining changes in repertoires of contention and vice versa. Recurrent processes and mechanisms are highlighted. This approach is rooted in his original finding, reported in *Popular Contention in Great Britain* (1998), that social changes tied to capitalism, urbanization, and new technologies led to the rise of both the modern national parliament in Great Britain and the social movement. He shows how the relationship between ordinary people and powerholders changed through struggle during this period. In *Democracy* (2003) and *Trust and Rule* (2005), Tilly elaborates. He shows that most social movement activity takes place in relatively democratic and high-capacity regimes, not less democratic and weak regimes. By democratic, he means "the extent to which authorities consult in meaningful ways with all of their population equally and protect minority positions" (Tilly and Wood 2013: 128). According to Tilly, the sources of this pattern are relationships between powerholders and population, or what he calls "regime and repertoire."

From this point of view, democratic, high-capacity states like the United States and Canada are relatively open to challengers. They are places where social movements flourish. They enjoy rich histories of social movement struggle that have led to significant expansion of political rights and freedoms around gender, race, disability, and location over the past 60 years. However, things change. Democratization can be reversed as social relations and relationships to power change and as authorities become less accountable to, and less consultative with, the full breadth of the population.

Durable inequalities and declining democracy

Many observers have noted that neoliberal globalization has made a small number of people and companies enormously wealthy and thus transformed the relationship between states and populations. In particular, the state has an increasingly repressive relationship with racialized, low-income communities and an increasingly convivial and supportive relationship with wealthy White people. When this happens, politics becomes more fragmented along lines of race and class, with the state providing less economic security to, and less meaningful consultation with, racialized, Indigenous, poor, and rural people. In Tilly's words, the "weakening of barriers between categorical inequality and public politics, segregation of new or existing trust networks from public politics, and so on" shape the form of contention (Tilly and Wood 2013, 157).

There is good reason to believe that categorical inequalities—particularly race, class and urban/rural divides—are affecting politics and fragmenting trust networks. First, while the dominant narrative of human rights and democracy prevails in Canada and the United States, after 50 years of increase, the proportion of countries described as democratic has stalled (Freedom House 2018). Second, we know that income inequality is increasing in most countries, as is debt and housing unaffordability. Third, tension is mounting between the rhetoric of democracy and the capitalist individualism of the North American dream. Such tensions are mobilized by social movements. We see this in the populist phrasing of Occupy Wall Street ("the 99% vs. the 1%"), the Tea Party ("Crooks in Washington") and Trump ("Drain the Swamp"), and in the highlighting of unfulfilled liberal promises of human rights and equity by Black Lives Matter and No One Is Illegal.

Such durable inequalities are exacerbated by changes in communications media. The print newspaper is in decline as readership and advertising dollars fall. More people obtain information through selective, narrow-casted social media that tend to confirm existing biases (Gottfried and Shearer 2017). This phenomenon is tied to shifts from a social life that is ascribed by location, family, and career to one of choice or "networked individualism" (Wellman 2001). Fewer shared, socially heterogeneous sites of interaction exist (Putnam 2000).

These developments coincide with declining trust in public institutions and authorities. According to Gallup Historical Trends (2018), Americans who have "a great deal/quite a lot" of trust in Congress declined from 42 percent in 1973 to 9 percent in 2016. For the Presidency, we see a drop from 72 percent in 1991 to 36 percent in 2016; and for big business, from 26 percent to 18 percent over the same period. The decline in trust is dramatic in the United States but it is evident in Canada too (Edelman Trust Barometer 2018). In both countries, it is shaped by growing categorical inequalities of race, class, citizenship, urban/rural differences, gender, religion, and ethnicity. As the importance of these inequalities have increased and become more distinct, people are fragmented into more homogeneous, and more self-consciously homogeneous clusters.

Alongside such fragmentation, changes to contentious politics occur, suggesting that the changes in contention that Tilly predicted are indeed shaped in part by categorical inequalities. People who operate in a professionalized, internationalized, and cosmopolitan global arena through non-governmental organizations and transnational social movements are likely to be categorically different from those who continue to participate in classic social movements with their ongoing campaigns, displays of worthiness, unity, numbers and commitment, and repertoires oriented toward making demands on the state. People who wish to build alternatives to state-oriented policy and practice operate differently.

Of course, these categories are neither fixed nor impermeable.

Some movements bring people together across social divides and combine contentious strategies. Someone's class or racial identity does not determine one's contentious strategy. Sometimes the wealthiest ally with the poorest. However, given that people tend to favour the methods that are identified with, and seen as effective and appropriate to, their own trajectories, a correlation exists between durable categorical inequalities, relationships with authorities, and contentious strategies.

Tilly thought that people excluded from the state would operate increasingly outside it, at the local level and/or within subsections of political relations, using other tactics and forms of action. He notes: "Segments of the population that withdraw their trust networks from public politics, weaken their own interest in governmental performance, hence their zeal to participate in democratic public politics" (Tilly 2005: 114). He is not alone in noting that many claimants do not trust the state to address their demands through campaigns and displays of worthiness, unity, numbers, and commitment. Indeed, many authors note that with neoliberal globalization, many people become cynical about the "social movement society." While activists may continue to use conventional methods to make demands on the state, they often combine them with the establishment of "prefigurative" organizations and social relations that reflect the world activists are trying to create (Dixon 2014). We can see such diversity in contentious strategy. In 2016, the most visible movements were those organized by people marginalized by racism and colonialism arguing that they are not just protesters but seekers of "collective liberation" (Movement for Black Lives), some as "Water Protectors" (Standing Rock) or "Land Defenders" (Unist'ot'en camp). Through the year, struggles led by Black and Indigenous groups made these state-averse strategies particularly visible.

However, sometimes shocks to the system occur. Things destabilize. Economic, political, social, and ecological crises or even elections can destabilize relations and elites. Sections of elites may become, or seem to become, more open to challengers, encouraging and building relationships with grassroots actors. Social movement scholars describe these circumstances as political opportunities or threats. Alimi and Hirsh-Hoefler (2012: 331) tie the emergence of a counter-movement to the structure of political opportunities and threats. They define threat as "consistent, although not necessarily institutional, formal, or permanent dimensions of the political environment, that encourage or discourage the movement from engaging in contention by altering its strategic position and hence its ability to exercise political leverage in a favorable or an unfavorable manner" (Alimi and Hirsh-Hoefler 2012: 332). The election of Trump is just such a moment.

Method and data

To sketch the effects of the Trump election on protest in North America, I examined protest activity in 2016 and 2017. Specifically, I used *New York Times* and *Globe and Mail* coverage of protests in Canada and the United States to build catalogues of protest events in the two countries. I recognize that this method captured only a fraction of overall protest activity and an even smaller selection of social movement or contentious activity. However, research has shown that newspapers tend to cover conflictual, large protests tied to the larger news cycle relatively consistently across time (Oliver and Maney 2000; Smith et al. 2001). While the *New York Times* is consistently used as a source in event catalogues tracking US protests, Wilkes and Ricard (2007) show that there is no single equivalent source in Canada. However, they do find that *Globe and Mail* coverage does reflect the overall ebb and flow of protest. My search terms were "protesters," "protested," and "protest." Once I identified an event in the newspaper, I added detail to the entry using a Google search, and searches of Facebook and Twitter.

Table 1 summarizes my findings. It suggests five main observations. First, in the United States, there was a large increase in the number of protests from 2016 to 2017. Second, many mobilizations and campaigns persisted over the two years. Third, despite an ongoing and central focus on race and migration, shifts occurred in the issues of protest from 2016 to 2017 and in Canada/United States differences in the focus of protests. Fourth, right-wing mobilizations increased in both countries in 2017. Fifth, movement/countermovement interactions increased in 2017.

The first three observations are straightforward; we would expect cross-time and cross-national contexts to affect protest patterns. We would also expect the political party in power to matter. The Trump election created a political opportunity for the right and a political threat to the left. On the left, it mobilized a broad array of actors, including many from the broader liberal left who did not regularly engage in street protest during the Obama era—including the National Association for the Advancement of Colored People (NAACP), the Democratic Party, PEN and the American Civil Liberties Union (ACLU). Trump's election stimulated more right-wing protest in Canada and the United States, sending signals to far-right activists who sought to move the public debate even further to the right. Trump amplified a message of nationalism, xenophobia, and sexism that right-wing grassroots activists took up.

Moving beyond the newspaper data, there was also a shift in the type of right-wing formations active in the United States and Canada. Between 2016 and 2017, the Southern Poverty Law Center found that the number of hate groups in the US rose by 4 percent, from 892 to 917. Anti-Muslim groups grew by 13 percent, anti-immigrant groups by 14 percent, patriot groups by 10 percent, and neo-Nazi groups by 22 percent. New organizations and chapters formed, with alt-right groups like the Patriot Front, the Fraternal Order of the Alt Knights, Identity Europa, and Vanguard America expanding. Hate crimes also increased, with the *New York Times* reporting that overall hate crimes jumped 17 percent in 2017, with a 37 percent increase in crimes against Jews and Jewish institutions (Weisman 2019). A similar though less dramatic trend was evident in Canada (Brym 2019). There is no equivalent to the Southern Poverty Law Center in Canada, but online activity might offer some insight. Moonshot CVE, a UK-based counter-extremism and research outfit identified 5,214 far-right web searches in Canada between September 11 and 25, 2018. Eighty-eight percent of these searches focused on neo-Nazi and White supremacy websites. Search terms included David Duke, popular neo-Nazi phrases and code words, extreme right-wing bands, and tattoos of swastikas or similar imagery (Boutilier 2018a).

In Canada, like the US, most people have positive attitudes toward immigrants and immigration. Nonetheless, evidence of a rising anti-immigrant hard-right-wing exists. Barbara Perry found that between 2015 and 2018, there was a 20 to 25 percent jump in the number of right-wing extremist groups active in Canada, with 100 to 125 such organizations in 2018 (Boutilier 2018b). Successes appear to have opened space for even more right-wing movements to take to the streets to challenge what they perceive as left-wing, liberal, Muslim, or immigrant institutions, norms, and individuals.

The 2016 presidential election, existing movements, and ongoing durable inequalities opened political opportunities for right-wing movements and posed political threats for left-wing movements, exacerbating partisan divides between left and right, and reinforcing racial and national identities. This process coincided with shifts in contentious strategies and was evident in the names of groups involved in protests in Canada and the United States in 2016 and 2017. While the names of organizations alone cannot capture their contentious strategies, digging a little deeper and identifying different types of formation (e.g., coalition, formal organization), whether they operate locally or nationally, and the goals and framing of the campaign can help us understand the broad contentious strategies they utilized.

Overall, in both countries and in both years, one sees a mix of political parties, loose networks, anti- and pro-Trump coalitions (Bikers for Trump, Stand Together Against Trump), community organizations, NGOs like Greenpeace and groups that involve both online and offline elements. In the United States, national organizations like the ACLU and the NAACP played a more visible role, whereas local Indigenous and other communities were more visible in Canada. The only consistent actor in both years and in both countries was Black Lives Matter. In 2017, in both countries, we see organizations that are willing to engage in street confrontation, such as Proud Boys and Antifa. Fringe political parties on the left and the right became more visible in 2017, as did protests by inside-the-system formations like the Democratic Party and the New York Police Department.

In the United States, some liberal organizations returned to the streets after a long hiatus. While this dataset looked for public gatherings of claims making, that is, protest activity, most of the time these organizations engaged in institutionalized advocacy, policy work, labour negotiations, and electoral politics too. Some of them operated locally, others nationally, and some transnationally. A resurgent right wing was also new to street protest, fueled both by online activity and the confidence fostered by Trump.

Left-right interactions

One noteworthy feature of the rise of right-wing protest activity is an expansion of movement/counter-movement interaction. In 2016, there were scattered yelling matches between Trump supporters at rallies and activists protesting or attempting to disrupt the rallies. In 2017, such interaction expanded dramatically in both countries. Right-wing protesters almost always encountered left-wing counter-protesters. At all nine Marches Against Sharia in the United States in 2017 there was a left counter-mobilization, most of the time by Antifascists, sometimes identifying explicitly as Antifa.

We find interesting patterns underlying right-wing protests and left-wing counter-protests. If we exclude Trump opponents yelling and scuffling outside of Trump electoral rallies, the only evidence of right-left protest interactions in 2016 was in Chicago between supporters of Black Lives Matter and Blue Lives Matter, first triggered by the Mayor's decision to fly a Black Lives Matter flag at City Hall, and then exacerbated by the police shooting of Joshua Beal. In 2017, after Trump was elected, the number of events involving movements and counter-movements increased in both the United States and Canada until August. In February 2017, a day of pro-life protests was organized across 200 American cities by the Pro-Life Action League and the Catholic Church. In response, pro-choice counter-protests took place in thirteen cities identified by the *New York Times*. In April 2017, men's rights activists rallied in Georgia against a Sexual Assault Bill, and on Tax Day, April 15th, pro- and anti-Trump activists gathered outside the President's home in Mar-A-Logo, Florida. The same day, renamed Patriots Day, the alt-right mobilized in Berkeley with the Liberty Revival Alliance, the Oath Keepers, Biker groups, and the Proud Boys. They were opposed by a coalition of groups, although the media named only Antifa. Clashes resulted in thirteen arrests.

We can see two types of confrontations between left and right in the United States. The first type occurred in the southern cities of Charlottesville and New Orleans. They pivoted on the removal of statues of Confederate soldiers and leaders and brought existing local formations together with the alt-right networks. The *New York Times* identified four events in May in New Orleans, involving existing local actors, and three events in Charlottesville in July and August, the last being the "Unite the Right" confrontations that attracted activists from across the United States and Canada, in which one counter-protester was killed. The second cluster of events occurred in urban centres around universities in New York City and Berkeley and appeared to be driven more by alt-right networks. There was the "Patriots Day" rally in April in Berkeley, involving many alt-right players, an alt-right rally against a pro-Palestine speaker at City University of New York in May, a march against Sharia law in New York City in June, and a pro-Trump/anti-hate protest in Berkeley in August. In Canada, the movement/counter-movement interactions were small and involved far-right groups making claims against Muslim immigration in Calgary and Toronto. After Charlottesville, these confrontations disappear. Nonetheless, in the spring and summer of 2017, right protest/left counter-protest confrontations around religion, race, and immigration were particularly common in relatively progressive centres with relatively progressive municipal governments and longstanding left-wing and anti-racist movements. These cities also had visible alt-right formations, on- and offline, the most visible of which were the Proud Boys and Antifa.

Table 3.1. Protests, United States and Canada, 2016–17

Year	Country			
	United States		**Canada**	
	Focus of protest	*Frequency*	*Focus of protest*	*Frequency*
2016	Anti Trump candidacy/ election	134	Anti Black racism[5]	11
	Anti Black racism	47	Pro Indigenous sovereignty	8
	Pro $15 minimum wage	18	Anti homelessness	5
	Anti pipelines	6	Anti Uber	3
	Pro White supremacy	4	Anti pipelines	2
	Anti Clinton candidacy	4	All other issues[7]	14
	All other issues[1]	41		
	Subtotal	**254**	**Subtotal**	**53**
2017	Women's march	82	Anti immigrant[8]	19
	Pro immigrant[2]	45	Pro Indigenous sovereignty[9]	10
	Pro Affordable Care Act	35	Anti racism	6
	Anti Black racism[3]	27	Women's march/ anti Trump	6
	Anti Trump	27	All other issues[10]	7
	March against Sharia	17		
	Anti White supremacy	20		
	Anti racism	10		
	Anti abortion	15		
	All other issues[4]	161		
	Subtotal	**439**	**Subtotal**[11]	**48**
	Total	**693**	**Total**	**91**

1. All other issues are diverse—bear hunts, school closings, layoffs; includes four counterprotests.
2. Includes protests against executive order, Muslim ban, and end to sanctuary cities.
3. Includes protests against acquittal of police officers.
4. Includes 41 counterprotests and 22 right-wing protests.
5. Includes protests against police shootings and killings.
6. Includes protests against hydroelectric projects (Site C and Muskrat Falls).
7. Includes two right-wing protests, anti-GMO, animal rights.
8. Includes protests against Muslims, religious accommodation, and Islamophobia.
9. Includes sovereignty and the environment.
10. Includes animal rights, drug consumption, bridge development.
11. Includes 11 counterprotests and 13 right-wing protests.

Conclusion

In the context of fragmented online and offline trust networks and partisan, racialized, and national identities, the Trump election presented a political opportunity for right-wing actors and a threat for their left-wing counterparts. Like other movements, those on the right emerge and grow because actors perceive a political opening and have the resources and relationships to mobilize members and new recruits around a message, identity, and strategy. Counter-movements appear when they perceive a threat. The boundaries between Black and White, Indigenous and Settler, immigrant and citizen, and urban and rural have long shaped contentious politics in the United States and Canada. Although these countries are heralded as democracies and sites of boundless opportunity, durable categorical inequalities divide those who are able to influence politics from those who are excluded from power. With neoliberal globalization, the state has moved farther from trying to resolve these exclusions through redistribution and inclusion, neglecting meaningful categorical equity initiatives or accountability. This neglect, in combination with a fracturing of communications media, has important consequences. Trust in public institutions declines, partly displaced by the "in-group" trust within local, racial, local, and partisan networks. In 2016, this was clear, with visible mobilizations like Black Lives Matter, and Idle No More seeking to make demands on the state, and simultaneously build communities, networks, and institutions that were designed to transcend its colonial, capitalist, racist limits.

This work continues. However, electoral politics matters. The election of Trump opened political opportunity for the right and posed a threat to the left. Existing movements were joined by new actors and networks, online and offline. Large, traditional left-wing social movement mobilizations have occurred. The right is also increasingly using the classic social movement repertoire. However, at times and in some places, clashes occur between right and left.

These confrontations are not *sui generis*. They depend on the existence of local offline and online movements on the left and the right that are connected locally, nationally, and sometimes internationally. Such clashes tend to happen in contexts that have a left-wing municipal government and a local trigger. This analysis complicates the usual narratives mentioned at the beginning of this paper about online movements, the displacement of left-wing street protest by right-wing street protest, and brawling.

What does this analysis suggest about the future of social movements in Canada and the United States? The decline of democracy in these increasingly unequal societies, together with the growing importance of international professional NGOs and transnational movements, weakens the relationship between politics and many people's day-to-day lives. At the same time, the Internet facilitates instability, with the construction of new collective identities, diffusion of tactics and frames, and rapid mobilization of movement symbols. This has meant that there has been a diversification of contentious strategies. Some people on the left and the right continue to use the social movement repertoire and make claims on the state. Others join formations organized around racial, Indigenous, local or partisan trust networks and seek to resolve politics outside the state, building communities of self-defence (fight clubs, unions, cooperatives, networks, and so on). This process sometimes involves prefigurative institution- and community-building strategies and sometimes involves a competitive, defensive, and confrontational strategy.

In a world where ordinary people, especially poor people and people of colour, are increasingly cynical about politicians and elites who talk about democracy and consultation without increasing equity and redistribution, trust is low and frustration high. The Trump election has led many people in the United States and Canada to continue rallying and marching in record number. Others expect less and less from those in charge. As Tilly noted, the future of social movements is uncertain. However, this paper suggests that, in a declining democracy, social movements continue, but their lack of purchase means they are joined by new strategies that involve building, experimenting, and confronting. While clashes can be seen as a sign of despair, they can also be seen as a sign of hope and determination to create a better world.

References

Alimi, E.Y., and Hirsh-Hoefler, S. 2012. Structure of political opportunities and threats, and movement-countermovement interaction in segmented composite regimes. *Comparative Politics* 44(3): 331–49.

Boutilier, Alex. 2018a. Rise of right-wing extremists presents new challenge for Canadian law enforcement agencies. *Toronto Star.* October 7. https://www.thestar.com/news/canada/2018/10/07/rise-of-right-wing-extremists-presents-new-challenge-for-canadian-law-enforcement-agencies.html.

Boutilier, Alex. 2018b. Web of hate. *Toronto Star,* October 9: A1.

Brym, Robert. 2019. Anti-semitic and anti-Israel actions and attitudes in Canada and internationally: A research agenda. *Patterns of Prejudice* 53 (3).

Brym, Robert, Anna Slavina, Mina Todosijevic, and David Cowan. 2018. Social movement horizontality in the Internet age? A critique of Castells in light of the Trump victory. *Canadian Review of Sociology* 55(4): 624–34.

Castells, Manuel. 2012. *Networks of Outrage and Hope.* Oxford:: Polity.

Dixon, Chris. 2014, *Another Politics.* Berkeley, CA: University of California Press.

Edelman Trust Barometer. 2018. https://www.edelman.ca/sites/default/files/2018-02/2018-Edelman-Trust-Barometer-Canada_ENGLISH.PDF.

Freedom House. 2018. *Freedom in the World: Democracy in Crisis.* https://freedomhouse.org/report/freedom-world/freedom-world-2018.

Gallup Historical Trends. 2018. Confidence in institutions. http://news.gallup.com/poll/1597/confidence-institutions.aspx.

Gerbaudo, Paulo. 2012. *Tweets and the Streets.* London: Pluto.

Gottfried, Jeffrey and Elisa Shearer. 2016. News use across social media platforms. Pew Research Center. http://www.journalism.org/2016/05/26/news-use-across-social-media-platforms-2016/.

Lind, Dara and Libby Nelson. 2016. 7 reasons everyone is so worried about violence in Cleveland. *Vox,* July 18. https://www.vox.com/2016/7/18/12200426/cleveland-republican-convention-violence.

Oliver, Pamela E. and Gregory M. Maney. 2000. Political processes and local newspaper coverage of protest events: From selection bias to triadic interactions. *American Journal of Sociology* 106(2): 463–505.

Perry, Barbara and Ryan Scrivens. 2016. Uneasy alliances: A look at the right-wing extremist movement in Canada. *Studies in Conflict and Terrorism* 39(9): 819–41.

Putnam R.D. 2000. *Bowling Alone: The Collapse and Revival of American Community.* New York: Simon & Schuster.

Smith, Jackie, John D. McCarthy, Clark McPhail, & Boguslaw Augustin. 2001. From protest to agenda building: Description bias in media coverage of protest events in Washington, D.C. *Social Forces* 79(1): 1397–1423.

Smith, Jackie, Samantha Plummer, and Melanie M. Hughes. 2017. Transnational social movements and changing organizational fields in the late twentieth and early twenty-first centuries. *Global Networks* 17(1): 3-22.

Southern Poverty Law Center. 2017a. Hate groups increase second consecutive year as Trump electrifies radical right. https://www.splcenter.org/news/2017/02/15/hate-groups-increase-second-consecutive-year-trump-electrifies-radical-right.

Southern Poverty Law Center. 2017b. *2017: The Year in Hate and Extremism.* https://www.splcenter.org/fighting-hate/intelligence-report/2018/2017-year-hate-and-extremism

Tarrow, Sidney. 2005. *The New Transnational Activism.* Cambridge, UK: Cambridge University Press

Tilly, Charles and Sidney Tarrow. 2015. *Contentious Politics,* 2nd ed. New York: Oxford University Press.

Tilly, Charles.1999. *Durable Inequality.* New Haven, CT: Yale University Press.

Tilly, Charles. 1998. *Popular Contention in Great Britain.* Cambridge, MA: Harvard University Press

Tilly, Charles. 2006. *Regimes and Repertoires.* Chicago: University of Chicago Press.

Tilly, Charles. 2005. *Trust and Rule.* Cambridge, UK: Cambridge University Press.

Tilly, Charles. 2003. *Democracy.* Cambridge, UK: Cambridge University Press.

Tilly, Charles and Lesley J. Wood 2013. *Social Movements: 1768–2012.* Boulder, CO: Paradigm/Routledge.

Tufekci, Zeynep. 2017. *Twitter and Tear Gas: The Power and Fragility of Networked Protest.* Yale University Press.

Weisman, Johnathan. 2019. American Jews and Israeli Jews are headed for a messy breakup. *New York Times.* January 4. https://www.nytimes.com/2019/01/04/opinion/sunday/israeli-jews-american-jews-divide.html.

Wellman, Barry. 2001. The rise of networked individualism. In *Community Networks Online* (pp. 17–42), Leigh Keeble (Ed.). London: Taylor & Francis.

Wilkes, Rima and Danielle Ricard. 2007. How does newspaper coverage of collective action vary? Protest by Indigenous people in Canada. *Social Science Journal* 44: 231–251.

CHAPTER FOUR
"Regroup, Recharge, Resist": How Modern Activists Mobilize in Difficult Contexts

Catherine Corrigall-Brown

The problem and its significance

Donald Trump was inaugurated on January 20, 2017. The next day, activists assembled in least 408 marches across the United States to express their unhappiness with the new president and his agenda (WomensMarch.com 2017). These marches were unprecedented in size, bringing together between 3.3 and 5.3 million Americans, or about 1 percent to 1.6 percent of the US population (Chenoweth 2017). At least 168 allied marches took place outside of the United States, bringing an additional 2 to 3 million participants to the cause (WomensMarch.com 2017). This international mobilization included 29 marches in Canada. While these events were predominantly populated by women, they brought together a wide diversity of activists interested in a variety of issues, including women's rights, reproductive rights, immigrant rights, civil rights, LGBTQ rights, the environment, government accountability, workers' rights, and more.

This extraordinary level of engagement was inspiring to many on the left, who felt disheartened by the results of the election and passionate about a more progressive agenda. However, activists who experienced the elation of the mass mobilization were quickly worried that it would be difficult to sustain this high level of engagement until the midterm elections of 2018 and the next presidential election of 2020.

The organization, Indivisible, was formed in an attempt to sustain the enthusiasm of the mass mobilization. Indivisible is a non-profit organization that aims to bring together local volunteer-led groups that engage in progressive advocacy and electoral work at the local, state, and national level (Indivisible.org 2018). The national organization supports local Indivisible groups and offers legislative advocacy and policy expertise. It also provides an online tool to help potential activists find others in their area who want to engage in progressive mobilization.

I conducted a project that followed 31 Indivisible groups founded in 10 cities immediately after the 2017 March. These include five cities with relatively conservative contexts and five cities in comparatively liberal areas matched on population size. I begin this paper by examining all activities and events listed on the Facebook pages of the 31 groups, almost 4,000 events from January 2017 to January 2018. I systematically collected data on the number of participants and comments per event and elements of the event itself such as the tactics used, coalitional ties, and framing.

I use these data to answer two main research questions. First, what predicts the level of mobilization and survival of online protest groups? Second, how does the political context influence which groups survive and mobilize over time? By systematically comparing engagement and events in five cities in politically conservative areas and five cities in politically liberal areas, I assess how political context shapes mobilization and the ability of groups to survive. I find that liberal areas have more and larger events on average. However, contrary to what we might expect, groups in conservative areas are more likely to survive over time, as measured by whether they are still hosting events after one year.

The second part of this paper focuses on a comparison of six Indivisible groups in two cities, Dayton, Ohio and Salt Lake City, Utah. These cities are of similar size and both have a conservative political landscape. However, Salt Lake City enjoyed a much higher levels of mobilization. In addition, all three of the Salt Lake City groups were still active after one year. Dayton was much less active and only one of the three Indivisible groups was still hosting events after the first year. Comparing these two cities allows me to identify the factors that are associated with group survival and mobilization within relatively conservative political environments. I argue that three main factors predict a high level of engagement and survival in less conducive contexts: coalitions, bridging the political/non-political divide, and reducing barriers to action. I begin by examining the literature on online activism, coalitions, and participation in movements.

Mobilizing online

Online mobilization has been described as both the saviour and the death of social movement activism. It has also provided challenges to social movements scholars as they attempt to make sense of it. This is in part because the diversity in forms of online organizing and engagement tests our ability to compare these campaigns with the offline mobilizations that both preceded and exist alongside it.

The first challenge in assessing online activism is making sense of its complexity and diversity. Online activism is not all the same. Earl et al. (2011) delineate four types of online engagement. First, brochureware uses technology to spread information online, but not to invite or enable participation. Second, e-mobilizations use online tools to facilitate offline protest. Third, online participation is engagement in online activities such as online petitions. Finally, online organizing of e-movements uses online tools to wholly organize movement efforts online (Earl and Kimport 2011). The present study focuses on e-mobilizations and online participation.

Clearly, some forms of online engagement are just extensions of what we are familiar with in face-to-face protest. However, other forms of online engagement, particularly online participation and online organizing, are fundamentally different (Earl and Kimport 2011). These forms of online activism can be used to radically reduce the costs of participating and organizing (Earl and Kimport 2011). In addition, the Internet can be used to dramatically increase coordination capacity across time and space when compared with face-to-face organizing. That is because the Internet can facilitate coordination across a broad group of people without requiring them to come together physically. It can also allow people to organize protest campaigns on their own or in small groups.

Online activism may also differ in its capacity to sustain itself. This is one of the core concerns of this chapter. Many scholars have argued that online social movements are episodic by nature. Bennett and Fielding (1999), for instance, introduced the idea of online "flash activism." The standard model of "power in movement" has been that the power of social movements springs from enduring social challenges (Tarrow 1994). From this perspective, the consistency of challenge is one of its most fundamental elements. However, online activism can gain power from its quick but overwhelming force. Many researchers have illustrated this tendency for rapid mobilization and de-mobilization online (Earl and Kimport 2011; Earl and Schussman 2002, 2004; Gurak 1997, 1999; Gurak and Logie 2003; Schussman and Earl 2004). It is important to note that the short-lived nature of some online campaigns is not necessarily related to their success. However, it does highlight one potential difference between on- and off-line activism.

The role of coalitions and social ties
Online activism often involves the use of coalitions, or alliances between social movement organizations. The extent of cooperation

between social movement organizations varies by degree, time, and scope (Tarrow 2004). Variation in degree refers to differences in the extent to which groups endorse the efforts and claims of other groups by offering them attention and/or resources. The second dimension of cooperation is temporal. Groups may cooperate for a one-time event or may coordinate a campaign that lasts years. Finally, inter-group affiliation may involve cooperation over single or multiple political issues. In the latter case, the coalition typically becomes a distinct organization, with independent staff, membership, and fundraising (Corrigall-Brown and Meyer 2010).

The choice to participate in a coalition carries potential costs and benefits, partly dependent on the nature and extent of participation. For example, cooperation among groups increases the visibility of the movement and its chance of being effective. Additionally, a broad coalition affords the prospect of mobilizing a wide range of people, adopting a multitude of tactics, and entering a large number of institutional niches. Multiple organizations in coalition also allow a movement to escalate despite setbacks faced by a single organization (McAdam 1983). At the same time, single organizations can specialize in terms of issues and tactics, enhancing not only the profile of the movement but also its flexibility (Staggenborg 1986).

Coalition participation can also carry risks. By cooperating with groups that may appeal to the same funders or members, an organization may obscure its own identity in service of a larger movement or its capacity to recruit members or raise funds (Rohlinger 2002). Organizations cultivate distinct organizational identities that define them to members and the outside world (Clemens 1993). These identities encourage certain alliances while forestalling others. Alliances can compromise identities and visibly associate organizations with unreliable or tainted allies (Haines 1988; Van Dyke 2003).

External circumstances alter the costs and benefits of cooperation (Meyer 2004). Researchers have examined contextual factors that affect the calculus of cooperation. For instance, in an historical study of the suffrage movement, McCammon and Campbell (2002) examine alliances between suffragettes and the Women's Christian Temperance Union. They find that alliances are most likely to form in response to political threats, including mobilization and organization of the opposition (in this case, brewers' associations) and the prospect of legislative defeats. Similarly, in a longitudinal study of student activism across a wide range of American campuses, Van Dyke (2003) finds that both proximate (campus-based) and national threats spurred cooperation among a broad range of activist groups.

Social movement activities are usually embedded in dense relational settings. The probability that individuals will join an organization depends on the number and strength of social network ties that connect group members to each other and to nonmembers (Diani 2005; McPherson et al. 1992). In this way, integration into structural networks pulls individuals into social movements. For this reason, individuals who are integrated into their community are more likely to engage in protest than are others (McAdam 1986; Meyer and Corrigall-Brown 2005; Corrigall-Brown and Meyer 2010; Useem 1998).

What predicts the level of mobilization and survival of online protest groups? How does the political context influence which groups survive and mobilize over time? I turn to these questions after outlining this study's methodology.

Methods

In February 2017, a month after the Women's March, I collected a list of all Indivisible groups in ten US cities. I selected five cities that were in politically conservative areas and five in politically liberal areas. I coded cities as conservative or liberal based on two factors: the political party of the state senators and the percentage of the vote that went to Trump in the 2016 election (see the Appendix). I selected cities that range in population size—four have large populations ranging from 300,000 to 640,000 and six have medium-size populations ranging from 140,000 to 200,000. I also selected cities that represent major regions in the United States (East Coast, West Coast, Midwest, and South). The cities are listed in Table 4.1.

Table 4.1. Cities by political context and population size

Political context	Medium	Large
Conservative	Amarillo, Texas Dayton, Ohio Salt Lake City, Utah	Atlanta, Georgia Pittsburgh, Pennsylvania
Liberal	Bridgeport, Connecticut Pasadena, California Springfield, Illinois	Newark, New Jersey Portland, Oregon

Thirty-one Indivisible groups in the ten cities were listed on the Indivisible website. It is important to note that groups other than these 31 engaged in progressive activism in these cities. However, this sampling technique allowed me to systematically select all groups that signed up for the Indivisible search engine and track their activities and survival over time.

I collected all information on the events and activities of the 31 groups over the first year of mobilization—until the second annual Women's March in January 2018—as listed on the group Facebook pages. I also determined whether the groups were still active in January 2018. For each event, I coded the date and time of the event, the number of hours it lasted, the number of comments it elicited, the number of people who attended it, the tactic used, and the use of coalitions. I also coded the event summaries and comments in order to analyze the mobilization in Salt Lake City, Utah, and Dayton, Ohio, in more depth.

Findings
Mobilizing in conservative and liberal contexts

Mobilizing people to action is often challenging. For several reasons, we would expect mobilization to be especially difficult for progressive movements in conservative contexts. First, there are by definition fewer liberal or progressive people in a conservative environment. Second, in a more conservative environment we would expect groups to have few political and other allies, such as elected officials or other civic leaders who are sympathetic and allied to their cause. Finally, in more conservative areas, we would expect there to be a weak tradition of progressive activism on which movements could draw. Taylor's (1989) work on abeyance structures highlights how movements can re-energize past activists or organizations after mobilization lulls. In conservative areas, we would expect fewer such individuals and organizations.

To assess the role of city political context, I compared five cities in liberal areas with five in conservative areas. In the first year after Trump was inaugurated, more groups were founded in the conservative cities than in the liberal cities (19 versus 17 groups). However, the Indivisible groups were much more active in the liberal areas than in the conservative areas. In more liberal cities, there was an average of 1.58 events per 1,000 residents with 207 people attending each event (see Table 4.2). The most active city was Pasadena, with 5.46 events per 1,000 population and average of 680 people attending each event. Bridgeport also had a large number of events, with 4.35 events per 1,000 population and an average of 140 attendees. Portland had fewer events (0.89 per 1,000 population) but they were well attended with an average of 179 attendees per event. Mobilization in Newark and Springfield was much lower.

Conservative areas tended to exhibit less mobilization. They had an average of 1.14 events per 1,000 population with 147 attendees.

Table 4.2. Mobilization by political context

City	Conservative			City	Liberal		
	Events per 1,000 population	Mean attendance	Group survival		Events per 1,000 population	Mean attendance	Group survival
Pittsburgh	0.71	143	3/5 (60%)	Bridgeport	4.35	140	2/2 (100%)
Salt Lake City	3.21	160	3/3 (100%)	Newark	0.41	10	1/2 (50%)
Dayton	0.17	94	1/3 (33%)	Springfield	0.36	27	3/3 (100%)
Amarillo	0.32	63	2/2 (100%)	Pasadena	5.46	680	2/3 (66%)
Atlanta	1.22	148	6/6 (100%)	Portland	0.89	179	2/7 (29%)
Average	1.14	147	79% (15/19)		1.58	207	59% (10/17)

Salt Lake City enjoyed a high level of mobilization, with 3.21 events per 1,000 population and 160 attendees. In fact, Salt Lake City was the third most active city despite its conservative political landscape. Pittsburgh and Atlanta had fewer events (0.71 and 1.22 per 1,000 population, respectively) but a relatively high number of attendees, with an average of 143 people attending each event. The other conservative cities, Dayton and Amarillo, had much lower levels of mobilization.

I also measured group survival by assessing whether groups were still active after one year of mobilization. Counter to expectations, Indivisible groups in conservative areas were much more likely to be active after one year than were groups in liberal areas. Seventy-nine percent of groups in conservative areas (15/19) were still active after one year while only 59 percent of groups in liberal areas (10/17) were still hosting events after one year.

While liberal areas have larger and more frequent events, they are less likely to be able to sustain groups over time. It is possible that liberal areas are able to attract members more easily because of the larger supply of sympathetic audiences and a more conducive political context. Conservative areas clearly have more difficulty fostering activism. However, in conservative contexts with relatively high barriers to action, people who become involved are more apt to sustain their groups over time. In the next section, I compare two conservative city contexts, one which was very active and one which was much less active. This comparison allows me to identify the processes that lead to mobilization and sustained action in conservative contexts.

Salt Lake City, Utah, and Dayton, Ohio

Preliminary analysis at the city level provides insight into mobilization across political contexts. While liberal cities have more and bigger events, conservative cities are more able to sustain their engagement over time. Three factors enable groups in conservative contexts to sustain mobilization: intensely engaging in coalition work, tying political to non-political issues and events, and facilitating the engagement of new activists by reducing barriers to action.

To illustrate the importance of these factors for group survival, I compare Dayton and Salt Lake City. Both cities are conservative and of similar size. Three Indivisible groups formed in each city. Salt Lake City held 3.21 events per 1,000 population with an average of 160 attending (see Table 4.3). All three groups were active at the end of the first year. However, Dayton held only 0.17 events per 1,000 population with only 94 people attending each event on average. Only one of the three groups was active after the first year.

Table 4.3. Comparison of Salt Lake City and Dayton

City	Group survival	Events per 1,000 population	Mean attendance	Events involving coalitions (percent)
Salt Lake City	3/3	3.21	160	91
Dayton	1/3	0.17	94	0

Salt Lake had three Indivisible groups. As Table 4.4 shows, Salt Lake 1 was most engaged, with 270 events and 1620 hours of activity, followed by Salt Lake 3 with 182 events and 746 hours of activity, and Salt Lake 2 with 170 events and 585 hours of activity. The events attracted a large number of people. An average of 530 people expressed interest in or attended Salt Lake 1 events, compared to 688 for Salt Lake and 518 for Salt Lake 3. Online commentary per event ranged from an average of 15 comments for Salt Lake 3 to 27 for Salt Lake 2. These results indicate that mobilization was occurring both on- and off-line in Salt Lake City.

Dayton also had three Indivisible groups, but none was highly active. Dayton 1 and Dayton 2 both hosted ten events and Dayton 3 listed four events in the first year. Dayton 1 had the largest number of people interested or going, with 656 engaging on average. On average, Dayton 2 and 3, respectively, had only eleven and four people attending each event. There was also much less online engagement in Dayton. Dayton 1 enjoyed 35 comments per event on average, but Dayton 2 and 3 elicited fewer than one comment per event. In Dayton, engagement was centred in one group and there was no community of Indivisible organizations in that city.

Three factors encouraged widespread engagement in Salt Lake City despite its conservativism. First, coalitions were formed by each of the city's Indivisible groups. Each event typically had many sponsors and involved cooperation with diverse civil society actors. Salt Lake 1 was the most active in this regard, with 97 percent of its events co-sponsored with other groups. Salt Lake 2 and Salt Lake 3 also engaged in coalition work for the great majority of their events—88 percent and 91 percent, respectively. In short, the Salt Lake groups rarely hosted events *without* coalition partners.

Moreover, the Salt Lake Indivisible groups cooperated with many different groups. Salt Lake 1 cooperated with 163 groups or individuals in their first year, Salt Lake 2 cooperated with 45, and

Table 4.4. Indivisible groups, Salt Lake City and Dayton

City/Group		Events					Facebook activity	
		Events	Hours	Average duration	Events involving coalitions (percent)	Mean attendance (range)	Mean in-teested (range)	Mean comments (range)
Salt Lake	1	270	1620	6.0	97	125 (0–4400)	405 (0–8300)	20 (0–716)
	2	170	585.2	3.4	88	210 (1–6800)	478 (0–16000)	27 (0–1105)
	3	182	746.2	4.1	91	174 (1–3100)	344 (0–2400)	15 (0–159)
Dayton	1	10	15.5	1.6	0	223 (0–1000)	433 (3–2500)	35 (0–182)
	2	10	19	1.9	0	3 (0–14)	8 (1–36)	0.1 (0–1)
	3	4	9.5	9.5	0	0.7 (0–2)	3 (0–7)	0.3 (0–1)

Salt Lake 3 cooperated with 141.

Notwithstanding the widespread use of coalitions, there were few *explicit* coalitions between the three Salt Lake Indivisible Groups. Salt Lake 1 and 2 never listed one another as coalition allies on an event and Salt Lake 2 only listed Salt Lake 3 as a co-sponsor for three events. However, there were many overlaps in shared ties to external groups. For example, Salt Lake 1 and 2 both cooperated with 15 of the same groups. Salt Lake 2 and 3 cooperated with 27 of the same groups. Salt Lake 1 and 3 were the most integrated, cooperating with 37 of the same groups. The groups that were linked to all three Indivisible organizations included the Salt Lake Public Library, Our Utah, Unidad Immigrante, Utah Indivisible, Utahs CD4 Coalition, Save Medicaid Utah, the ACLU, the Utah Sierra Club, and Utah Dine Bikeyah. There were also three individuals who hosted or co-hosted events with each of the three groups. Clearly, the Salt Lake activist scene involved a lot of cooperation across groups in progressive civil society. There were even a small number of events linked to by all groups, including the Women's March anniversary event, the March for Science, and a series of activities at the Salt Lake Library. The Indivisible groups in the city are an energetic part of this larger coalition of groups engaged in mobilizing in the area.

The Salt Lake City groups linked to the same events and allies more often in the first six months of the first year of mobilization and diverged in their actions and partners afterwards. After this initial period, they developed more distinct identities. Salt Lake 1 began focusing more on women's rights, Native Americans, and ties to the Democratic Party. Salt Lake 2 concentrated on environmental issues and parks. Salt Lake 3 focused on phone blitzes, postcard campaigns, and other activities aimed at influencing the votes of members of Congress.

In sharp contrast, the Indivisible groups in Dayton did not form coalitions. None of the groups ever co-hosted an event or engaged in formal coalition work. They never listed the same events across the Indivisible Facebook pages. Essentially, the groups worked in isolation from one another and separate from other civil society actors in Dayton.

Bridging the political/non-political divide

The three groups in Salt Lake City were effective at bridging the political/non-political divide. They did this by engaging with a variety of political institutions and groups inside and outside traditional politics. They also cooperated with apolitical civil society institutions such as libraries, universities, and charities. They engaged in actions that were political in nature, such as protests and town halls, but also in a variety of non-political activities, such as fundraisers for charities, parent-teacher events, and even events with business groups. In all these ways, the groups in Salt Lake were integrated with other groups and organizations in the city and were able to bridge the divide that sometimes exists between political and non-political action.

Specifically, Indivisible groups in Salt Lake City worked on a wide variety of issues, including LGBTQ rights, Native rights to land (particularly Bear Ear Park), the environment (particularly air quality), health care, education (including opposition to Betsy DeVos), racial inequality, the Muslim ban, homeless youth, reproductive rights, immigration (particularly refugees), and gun control.

These groups partnered with a wide range of civil society actors inside and outside traditional politics and social movement arenas. Salt Lake City 1, for example, co-hosted events with the Democratic party, candidates for office, government offices and city councils, and ran town halls with elected officials. They also engaged with social movement groups such as the Sierra Club, the ACLU, and Planned Parenthood. However, what is most interesting about the Salt Lake groups is their willingness to cooperate officially with non-political groups. For instance, they engaged extensively with the Salt Lake City library, which was active in putting on talks and courses to help individuals organize and engage in civil society. The library hosted a number of non-political events, such as an event about a new DUI law lowering the legal blood alcohol content level to 0.05 BAC (SLC 1, April 25). Salt Lake City 2 hosted a women's history month event moderated by a local radio host. The library panel included a librarian, Sandra Hollins (Utah State Representative, House District 23), the editor of the *Salt Lake Tribune*, a high school teacher, the program coordinator from Racially Just Utah, and a professor and associate vice president for equity and diversity at the University of Utah (February 22). Both events were focused on non-political issues but included political actors (such as elected officials and activists) to comment on issues. Salt Lake City 2 also hosted a totally non-political education event about wolf packs at Salt Lake City Public Library (November 2). These types of events brought out local residents to events where they could come in contact with Indivisible group members or their ideas.

The Salt Lake City groups also hosted events at the library where the topic bridged the political and non-political divide. For example, Salt Lake City 1 co-hosted a dialogue event at the library on how the county could cultivate a "sense of shared destiny and common civic purpose." The event was also a time to "inaugurat[e] Owl, our new county library mascot" (January 30). This event, held at a non-political location, tied a potentially political topic (dialogue on diversity) to a completely non-political event (a new library mascot). Other events were more obviously political in nature, such as Salt Lake City 1's course on using statistics for change, letter writing for change, and social media for change. This event sought to teach residents "how to engage and persuade in a positive and productive way ... to invoke social change" (February 4).

An event at a local neighbourhood house also connected political and non-political action. The house hosted a series of talks listed on Salt Lake City 1's Facebook page (March 30). The talks focused on creating a Neighborhood Watch association to reduce crime, starting a consulting business, making health and body products, chocolate and beer tasting, and lobbying for social change. The final event taught individuals how to engage in political lobbying, presented right after the beer-tasting night. Come for the beer, stay for the activism!

The Salt Lake City groups were also often engaged in non-political actions, such as the United Way campaign, cancer research fundraisers, suicide prevention, and school parent advisory groups. For example, Salt Lake City 1 hosted an "exciting service opportunity" providing hygiene kits for homeless people (January 30), an event on the opioid epidemic and suicide (June 10), and Tacofest to support Meals on Wheels (August 5). Salt Lake City 2 co-hosted a National Public Lands Day to "learn how to protect where you play and join your community in a day of wild appreciation for America's public land" (September 30).

The Salt Lake City groups cooperated with businesses, which some might consider unusual allies for groups on the political left. Salt Lake City 1 cooperated with Patagonia (March 7) and coordinated with business groups such as Womenpreneurs (April 4) and the Salt Lake Chamber Business Women's Forum (March 21). Salt Lake City 1 also hosted an event on January 31 that was sponsored by Zions bank—an "emerging leaders' initiative" aimed to get young professionals engaged in their community.

In sum, by engaging various segments of civil society, many of which were not political, Salt Lake City Indivisible groups broadened access to political work and destigmatized political engagement for people who might otherwise have been wary of progressive activism given the city's conservative context.

Dayton provided a very different context for mobilization. The three Indivisible groups in Dayton were mostly single-issue focused. Dayton 1 and 3 worked mainly on women's and reproductive rights (7 of 10 events and 2 of 4, respectively). Dayton 2 focused entirely on Democratic politics. The decision to work as a single- or multi-issue group is complex. There are benefits to focusing on one issue—it provides a clear identity and focus for the group, can attract members interested in the issue, and avoids some of the disagreements that come from members having different issue foci. However, being a single-issue group also brings disadvantages.

In general, the Dayton groups did not work on allied issues or expand their foci as the political context changed and new issues became central to public debate. Dayton 1 did host three events that were outside their core focus on women's rights. These events included "Demand an Independent Investigation" (May 10), "Fair Districts/Fair Elections" (August 6) and a Town Hall on Islamophobia and Racism (April 4). Dayton 3 also hosted two events unrelated to women's rights, an "Emergency Protest Against Trump's Refugee Ban" on February 3 and "Fire the Fool" on April 1. However, there was generally little connection between the actions of the Dayton Indivisible groups and issues beyond women's rights.

The Indivisible groups in Dayton did not work with coalition partners, thus remaining separate from the larger Dayton civil society. Dayton 1 did hold an event during which they discussed a possible collaboration for the People's Climate March. It would have involved a coalition with the Sierra Club. Later, there was no mention of the Sierra Club or the Climate March on the group's Facebook page. Future collaboration with the Dayton Women's Resistance was mentioned at a Dayton 1 meeting on October 22 and was noted in information about a film screening. However, the general lack of engagement with other groups was likely a critical factor leading to a low level of mobilization and group survival in Dayton.

Barriers to Entry
Facilitating action and first-timers
In conservative areas, fewer people engage in activism on the left or are available to mobilize. Therefore, movement groups must work to help convert non-activists into activists, motivate activists to engage, and/or reduce barriers to participation. The Salt Lake City groups worked energetically to accomplish all these goals.

The Salt Lake City groups engaged in much work to help people engage in first-time activism. Participating in activism for the first time can be intimidating; people might be concerned about social and political issues but do not know how to *do* activism. Salt Lake City groups facilitated first-time participation by engaging in a lot of activist training. A simple call, such as "Interested ... but don't know how to get involved?" conveys how much weight these groups put on trying to integrate new activists into their groups (SLC1, Jan. 30). Salt Lake City 1 explained that "If you have never lobbied before, don't worry. We will team you up with an experienced person and give you a quick training so you can see just how easy it really is" (February 1). Salt Lake City 2 also offered this type of training (April 21, April 27). These groups also worked more generally to educate potential activists, such as at an event where they focused on "taking questions as we help demystify our legislative process" (ALC2, May 30). Salt Lake City 2 offered workshops to help teach people how to write letters to the editor, phone a member of Congress, write persuasive op-eds, and support petitions.

The Salt Lake City groups considered the emotional challenges that first-time activists might face, such as the anxiety and socially awkward situations that they might encounter in the course of engagement. At one event, they explained that "We'll start with a training and end with a debriefing of our experience knocking on doors and talking to voters" (SLC2, April 27). Salt Lake City 1 also provided information on how to call a congressperson or senator when experiencing social anxiety (SLC 2, April 27).

The Salt Lake City groups worked to reduce the cost of engagement for new and experienced activists. For example, many events provided scripts for calling elected officials or for canvassing (SLC2 June 9, June 14). They also provided free postcards, clipboards, and stamps to facilitate engagement (SLC1, February 4). A November 5 "Postcards for America" event listed on Salt Lake City 2's website captures it best:

> We'll have cards, stamps, pens, even colored pencils if you want to get artsy. We recommend voicing your concerns to your member of Congress but, hey, we won't object if you write to a friend or even to your mom (or kid). Have an iced drink, eat a tasty homemade pastry, chat awhile, and make a difference. We'll be meeting the first Sunday of each month for the foreseeable future. All are welcome!

As this announcement makes clear, the cost of engagement will be low (all the materials and advice you need will be provided) and the level of enjoyment will be high (there will be food and jokes). In these ways, the Salt Lake City groups were facilitating engagement for new and continuing activists.

Another way the Salt Lake City groups encouraged activism was by highlighting multiple paths to engagement. Instead of simply calling for engagement in a protest, the groups went to great lengths to offer a variety of ways individuals could participate if they were unable or uninterested in participating in more contentious activities. Salt Lake City 1 co-sponsored a protest on December 12 and explained:

> We'd appreciate for you to spend your lunch break protesting with us, but there are multiple layers of participation! If you can't make the march, you can simply wear black and white in solidarity and/or take part in an [sic] spending moratorium from 12 to 12 on 12/12.

Other events noted: "Can't make it to the Monday sit-in? UAPB will also be conducting a call in" (SLC 1, January 30) and "If you cannot attend the meeting, please send a polite email" (SLC2, August 31). The Salt Lake City groups got creative about providing other forms of engagement, such as Salt Lake City 2's event where they introduced "resistbot" technology—a website where one can sign up and have a fax sent to one's congressional representative (April 27). In addition, many of the groups' events were livestreamed for those who could not attend.

Multiple pathways to engagement and training for new activists were especially prevalent in the first four months of mobilization in the Salt Lake City groups. After that, it seems, the groups had gained enough members and allies to focus less on recruiting new people and more on retaining them.

In general, much less information was provided about events on the Dayton Indivisible groups' Facebook pages. Event summaries were often only a few lines long, sometimes not even providing information on the location or time of an event. This practice restricted the opportunity to engage people who were new to activism by reducing barriers to action and identifying multiple ways to engage. One comment in November on Dayton 2's website captures it best: "Where do we go from here? We have many members and likes but few show up for meetings/events."

The Dayton groups occasionally discussed reducing barriers to action. For example, at one Dayton 1 event on February 11, organizers explained that they would have "other information about how to provide support and how to contact legislators ... including post cards to send." At the August 6 Dayton 1 meeting, organizers described information "about petition activities for Fair Districts=Fair Elections" and a brief training session followed the meeting. However, this practice was not widespread and was only evident at two of the 24 events in the city.

Conclusion

The election of Donald Trump was devastating for many on the political left. However, as I have demonstrated, it was also an important opportunity for mobilization. The massive and widespread events surrounding the Women's March in 2017 gave those on the left hope that they could resist some of the conservative agenda they feared. Many activists have sustained their engagement by participating in Indivisible groups. The research presented here highlights how critical events, such as elections, can provide powerful incentives for activists to mobilize. As Meyer and Staggenborg (1996) argue, political opportunities are not the only facilitators of mobilization—threats can also be powerful engines for social movements (see also Ramos and Wood in this volume).

In today's political environment, the political left faces multiple threats. In Canada, the federal government's purchase of the Trans-Mountain pipeline threatens environmental and Indigenous movements. The rise of political figures such as Doug Ford, François Legault, Maxime Bernier, and Faith Goldy threaten civil rights and immigrant groups to varying degrees. The present research highlights how social movements, even within conservative and less conducive contexts, can harness political threats to mobilize new and active citizens.

Today, social movements seem vibrant, with large-scale mobilizations by Black Lives Matter, Idle No More, Women's Marches, and environmental activists. However, mobilizations are difficult to sustain, limiting the possibility of creating lasting social change.

Tilly and colleagues considered how change in social movement mobilization may influence the future of social movements. They proposed four possible social movement futures (Tilly and Wood 2016). Social movements might shift to international targets and begin to organize at the international level; we may see a democratic decline that pushes social movements toward activities adapted to regional and local contexts; movements may embrace professionalization, shifting away from local and grassroots activism; and "people power" may lead to democratization and decentralization (Tilly and Wood 2016).

In this volume, Wood assesses these social movement futures by systematically examining mobilization on the left and right in Canada and the United States in 2016, before the election of Donald Trump, and in 2017, after his inauguration. She finds much more mobilization and counter-protest post-inauguration, which is consistent with the findings of my research. She also contends that democracy is in decline and that the Internet creates instability insofar as it facilitates both rapid mobilization and demobilization. I also find that online mobilization can be dramatic but short-lived. However, that is not always the case. Many of the groups I examined illustrate how online mobilization can be sustained.

My study also addresses Tilly's first assertion, namely that movements may become more international. The Women's March was the initial rapid mobilization that sparked the formation of the Indivisible groups I studied and it was international in scope. However, while the Women's March led to longer-term mobilization in much of the United States, it did not lead to sustained action in Canada and elsewhere. As Tilly argues, the democratic decline that Wood and Ramos discuss in this volume can push groups into adapting to their local or regional contexts. This certainly happened with the Women's March, which was less salient over time in countries such as Canada, which lacks a foil like Trump to stimulate mobilization. Other movements that are international in scope, such as Black Lives Matter, also tend to diverge over time in different local contexts as they struggle to make connections and highlight relevance to the local community.

Tilly's work also calls on us to assess the critical potential and pitfalls of professionalization for movements. Students of social movements have long debated the merits of professionalization—does it increase mobilization capacity or limit innovation and grassroots power? Among the groups I analyzed, professionalization and grassroots action work together in certain contexts. The impetus behind the development of the Indivisible website and organization was to bring expertise and professionalization to grassroots groups. However, instead of trying to make the groups the same in all contexts, the Indivisible website created resources like the tool that helps people find other local activists, and information such as guides to effective lobbying, canvassing, and hosting town halls. In the longstanding debate between the positive and negative potential of professionalization, it seems that modern groups are learning to professionalize, enjoying its benefits while avoiding its pitfall of stifling grassroots energy and engagement.

The Indivisible groups I analyzed show how modern activists can learn from past mistakes. They can harness the power of international mobilization for its dramatic and powerful message while sustaining action in local contexts. They can use the power and reach of Internet technologies to mobilize large groups quickly while also creating online communities to support action over time. They can harness resources and expertise to attract members to local groups that differ across contexts. Not all groups are equally able to navigate these difficult divides. Identifying what makes groups successful in these challenging contexts is critical for understanding how activists and movements can survive despite threats and uncertainty.

Appendix.
Coding of states as conservative or liberal

Political orientation	State	Percent Trump vote 2016 (Clinton vote)	Party of state senators
Conservative	Texas	52.2 (43.2)	2 Republican
	Ohio	51.7 (43.6)	1 Republican 1 Democrat
	Utah	45.5 (27.5)	2 Republican
	Georgia	51.3 (45.6)	2 Republican
	Pennsylvania	48.2 (47.4)	1 Republican 1 Democrat
Liberal	Connecticut	40.9 (54.6)	2 Democrat
	California	32.8 (61.6)	2 Democrat
	Illinois	38.8 (55.8)	2 Democrat
	New Jersey	41.4 (55.5)	2 Democrat
	Oregon	39.1 (50.1)	2 Democrat

References

Bennett, Daniel, and Pam Fielding. 1999. *Net Effect: How Cyberadvocacy is Changing the Political Landscape*. Merrifield, VA: E-advocates Press.

Chenoweth, Erica. 2017. This is what we learned by counting the women's marches. *The Washington Post*. https://www.washingtonpost.com/news/monkey-cage/wp/2017/02/07/this-is-what-we-learned-by-counting-the-womens-marches/?noredirect=on&utm_term=.efd-96fae7d07.

Clemens, Elisabeth S. 1993. Organizational repertoires and institutional change: Women's groups and the transformation of U.S. politics. *American Journal of Sociology* 98(4): 755–98.

Corrigall-Brown, Catherine and David S. Meyer. 2010. The pre-history of a coalition: An analysis of win without war. Pp. 3–21 in *Strategic Alliances,* edited by Nella Van Dyke and Holly McCammon. Minneapolis, MN: University of Minnesota Press.

Diani, Mario. 2005. Networks and participation. Pp. 339–59 in *The Blackwell Companion to Social Movements*, edited by David A. Snow, Sarah A. Soule and Hanspeter Kriesi. Malden, MA: Blackwell Publishing.

Earl, Jennifer and Katrina Kimport. 2011. *Digitally Enabled Social Change: Activism in the Internet Age*. Boston: MIT Press.

Earl, Jennifer and Alan Schussman. 2003. The new site of activism: On-line organizations, movement entrepreneurs, and the changing location of social movement decision making. *Research in Social Movements, Conflicts and Change* 24(1): 155–87.

Earl, Jennifer and Alan Schussman. 2004. Cease and desist: Repression, strategic voting, and the 2000 presidential election. *Mobilization* 9(2): 181–202.

Gurak, Laura J. 1997. *Persuasion and Privacy in Cyberspace: The Online Protests over Lotus MarketPlace and the Clipper Chip*. New Haven, CT: Yale University Press.

Gurak, Laura J. 1999. The promise and the peril of social action in cyberspace. Pp. 243-63 in *Communities in Cyberspace*, edited by Mark A. Smith and Peter Kollock. London: Routledge.

Gurak, Laura J. and John Logie. 2003. Internet protests, from text to web. Pp. 25–46 in *Cyberactivism: Online Activism in Theory and Practice*, edited by Martha McCaughey and Michael D. Ayers. New York: Routledge.

Haines, Herbert H. 1988. *Black Radicals and the Civil Rights Mainstream, 1954-1970*. Knoxville: University of Tennessee Press.

McAdam, Doug. 1986. Recruitment to high-risk activism—The case of Freedom Summer. *American Journal of Sociology* 92(1): 64–90.

McAdam, Doug. 1983. Tactical innovation and the pace of insurgency. *American Sociological* Review 48(6): 735–54.

McCammon, Holly J. and Karen E. Campbell. 2002. Allies on the road to victory: Coalition formation between the suffragists and the Woman's

Christian Temperance Union. *Mobilization: An International Journal* 7(3):231–51.

McPherson, J. M., P. A. Popielarz, and S. Drobnic. 1992. Social networks and organizational dynamics. *American Sociological Review* 57(2): 153–170.

Meyer, David S. 2004. Protest and political opportunity. *Annual Review of Sociology* 30: 125–45.

Meyer, David S. and Catherine Corrigall-Brown. 2005. Coalitions and political context: U.S. movements against wars in Iraq. *Mobilization* 10(3): 327–44.

Meyer, David, S. and Suzanne Staggenborg. 1996. Movements, counter-movements, and the structure of political opportunity. *American Journal of Sociology.* 101(6): 1628–60.

Rohlinger, Deana. 2002. Framing the abortion debate: Organizational resources, media strategies, and movement-countermovement dynamics. *Sociological Quarterly* 43(4): 479–507.

Schussman, Alan and Jennifer Earl. 2004. From barricades to firewalls? Strategic voting and social movement leadership in the Internet age. *Sociological Inquiry* 74(4): 439–63.

Staggenborg, Suzanne. 1986. Coalition work in the pro-choice movement. *Social Problems* 33(5): 374–389.

Tarrow, Sidney. 1994. *Power in Movement: Social Movements, Collective Action, and Politics.* New York: Cambridge University Press.

Tarrow, Sidney. 2004. *The New Transnational Activism.* Unpublished manuscript, Cornell University.

Taylor, Verta. 1989. Social movement continuity: The women's movement in abeyance. *American Sociological Review* 54(5): 761–75.

Tilly, Charles and Lesley J. 2016. *Social Movements: 1768–2012.* New York: Routledge.

Van Dyke, Nella. 2003. Crossing movement boundaries: Factors that facilitate coalition protest by American college students, 1930–1990. *Social Problems* 50 (2): 497–520.

Women's March. 2017. Sister marches. https://www.womensmarch.com/sisters.

CHAPTER FIVE

The Religious Right in Canada and the United States and Right-Wing Activism in Canada Today

Tina Fetner

Current events in Canada, as elsewhere in the world, point to a resurgence of populism, culturally and in electoral politics. It is characterized by increasingly vocal support of identity politics that celebrates traditional white masculinity, tapping into mainstream social values while advocating positions that include anti-Semitism, anti-gender equality, and anti-immigration. As Canadian electoral politics includes more candidates willing to test the waters of these divisive issues, scholars of right-wing activism and politics are called upon to focus their expertise on the current political moment. In that spirit, I offer insights from my comparative-historical research on religious right activism in Canada and the United States.

The research considers the historic cultural and policy differences that acted as "critical junctures" that placed Canadian conservative, evangelical Christians on a different path than their counterparts in the United States, putting them in a relatively weaker position to effect social change. Although today's populist resurgence is not directly tied to conservative evangelicalism or the religious right, the insights produced by this research project offer lessons for contemporary politics. For example, I consider whether the factors that produced differences in the strength and size of right-wing activism in the two countries historically are the same mechanisms that will influence Canada to move in a different direction than the United States, and indeed many parts of the global north, today.

In this moment of Brexit, Trump, and the rise of right-wing parties throughout Europe, can Canada rely on the same tools of bureaucratic control and cultural aversion to conflict that have been the hallmarks of Canada's difference from the United States thus far? I will argue that Canada's future is unclear precisely because these same mechanisms, while staving off the most extreme policy proposals from the religious right, have all along been in service of upholding a concept of Canada that valorizes whiteness and masculinity as authentic and natural. The cultural supports for white masculinity are strong in Canada, as they are in the UK, Europe and the United States, and the communities and organizations that support populist figures are understudied because they are somewhat hidden from our view.

To make this case, I will first present my argument as to how we got here by reviewing my historical-comparative research on the religious right in Canada and the United States, which offers lessons about the current state of Canadian politics. I then discuss what I perceive to be the heart of the problem of current right-wing cultural and political mobilizations by thinking through whether the mechanisms identified in my research—culturally ingrained politeness and bureaucratic control—can be successfully employed today to stave off right-wing mobilizations.

Data and method

My comparative case study relies on primary and secondary sources. Published historical analyses of evangelical Christianity in Canada and the United States, largely by historians and religious studies scholars, but also by a few sociologists, form the basis of many claims in my analysis. These sources are supplemented by government records, including census data, and surveys concerning religion in the 20th century. I have also collected original organizational data on religious right organizations to establish my claim that the United States religious right is larger and better funded than the Canadian religious right, a claim I pay more attention to elsewhere (Fetner forthcoming).

My analysis is based in historical institutionalism (Pierson and Skocpol 2002). This approach considers the path dependence of historical events, arguing that political actions taken at one point in time, such as the implementation of particular policies, shape options available to decision makers at later points in time. Thus, historical institutionalism seeks to identify moments when paths are embarked upon. These moments are "critical junctures" that shift a state's developmental path (Capoccia and Kelemen 2007). In this chapter, I identify two critical junctures that set Canadian evangelicals on a different historic path than their counterparts in the United States.

Both these critical junctures occurred in the 1920s, decades before anything that can be understood as a religious right social movement emerged and began its conservative, religious, mostly evangelical Christian political activism. However, the two moments produced profoundly different supports for the conservative, evangelical Christian communities in the two countries under examination. The different type of support shaped differences that matter to social movements, such as the size of the population from which supporters can be drawn, an organizational infrastructure to nurture ideas and develop leadership for a movement, a network of communications to inspire and mobilize supporters, and perhaps most importantly, a pool of financial resources to pay for the many expenses of mobilization. I argue that social movements scholars should pay more attention to historical forces to understand the promise of a social movement in its political and cultural context. I apply the insights gained from my historical research to a contemporary problem—the development of new right-wing mobilization in Canada.

Historical comparison of evangelical Christians in the United States and Canada

Like most scholars of the religious right, I identify the 1970s as the period of the movement's crystallization. The movement showed first signs of life in the form of single-issue counter-movements to two social movements in the 1960s: second-wave feminists and the lesbian and gay movement. Social movement organizations such as Phyllis Schlafly's Eagle Forum, Beverly LaHaye's Concerned Women for America, Anita Bryant's anti-gay group, Save Our Children, and the wave of anti-abortion organizations that emerged in response to the 1973 U.S. Supreme Court decision on Roe v. Wade can be considered immediate predecessors to the religious right. In the 1980s, Republican insiders worked with televangelist Jerry Falwell to create a broad, multi-issue, right-wing Christian movement represented by the Moral Majority organization. In Canada, right-wing organizations formed on a similar timeline. Campaign Life Coalition was established in 1978 to oppose the legalization of abortion. REAL Women of Canada was established in 1983 as an anti-feminist women's group. Focus on the Family Canada was established as an affiliate of the United States group in 1983.

However, from the outset the Canadian religious right was less successful at effecting social change than its American counterpart (Bean 2014). The pattern came into sharp relief when Stephen Harper was elected prime minister. Harper is a conservative, evangelical Christian, and his candidacy was supported by the Canadian religious right. He brought conservative, evangelical Christians into mainstream politics by leading the merger of the Progressive Conservatives with the more socially conservative Reform Party to produce the Conservative Party that he led and that exists today. It therefore makes sense to claim that Harper has been an important part of the religious right movement in Canada—if not a movement leader, then at least a key political ally of the movement. In his successful 2006 election campaign, he ran on a platform that opposed the recent legalization of same-sex marriage and carried much of the agenda of the religious right. However, once he was elected, and even when he led a majority government, Harper enacted little of the religious right agenda he campaigned on. Notably, he took no action on abortion or same-sex marriage policy despite his promises and personal views. Harper's political calculation was that these policy moves would be too risky for him to undertake, and the Canadian religious right was not strong enough to force his hand.

Organizational data supports Harper's cautious reading of the strength of the movement he helped put on the map. In a scan of religious right organizations, I found that there are far more organizations dedicated to activism aligned with religious right priorities in the United States than in Canada, even after accounting for population differences (Fetner forthcoming). Scholarship in the sociology of social movements has long understood that organizational support is important to the success of social movements (McCarthy and Zald 1977). Organizational resources can come from within movement organizations or they can exist as standalone institutions, with purposes distinct from the movements they support (Morris 1984). The stronger the organizations that support movements, the better the movements are able to take advantage of political opportunities and weather storms, and the likelier they are to survive over the long haul. Comparative approaches to institutional infrastructures reveal that not all institutional infrastructures are equally strong or supportive of movements (Desai 1996). The more that organizations facilitate contact among members, build community, and develop a sense of connection within a movement, the more useful the institutional infrastructure is to a movement.

At their heart, social movements are fundamentally shared ideas about social change, shared understandings of what constitutes social problems, a more-or-less agreed upon set of solutions for tackling those problems, and a shared set of goals for a future that aligns with a group's ideals. However, strong social movements, the ones that have potential to effect social change, are more than just ideas. Strong social movements have institutional infrastructures that support the development of their ideas, act as conduits for the spread of those ideas, and facilitate actions that can produce social change.

These resources include money and people, but also channels of communication and physical spaces in which people can gather. If the Canadian religious right had more of these, it likely would be more effective at producing social change. Prime Minister Harper would have felt empowered to make the policy changes that he personally supports. What happened in Canada to make the institutional infrastructure of the religious right so different from the United States?

To answer this question, I examined the history of evangelical Christianity in each country. I identified two critical junctures—historical moments when Canada and the United States embarked on different institutional paths. Each of them occurred in the 1920s, when the fundamentalist-modernist controversy was coming to a head throughout Christianity. The controversy called for churches and churchgoers to take a side on key issues, such as whether they would continue to believe that the Bible is the literal word of God, defining truth about the physical world around us, and whether modern forms of knowledge, like science, offer a better way to understand the world.

Critical juncture 1: Denominational shifts

The fundamentalist-modernist controversy hit American and Canadian evangelicals alike, but the results on evangelical Christian communities in the two countries were not the same. Scholars of religious history agree that, in the 1920s in the United States, evangelical Christians were fractured, having largely moved away from the denominations that previously housed them. Many stand-alone, independent churches emerged at this time, and the theology of many evangelicals was determined by local preachers rather than a denominational hierarchy. In addition, many evangelical Christian Americans grew distrustful of secular institutions and made a point of withdrawing from the secular world. Christian Smith (1998) argues that withdrawal was sometimes extreme, describing the doctrine of "double separation" that many evangelical Christians adopted: separation not only from people with modern beliefs, but also from anyone who would deal with such people. In short, the evangelical Christian community in the 1920s was large, fractured, and separatist.

In Canada, the evangelical Christian community did not look the same. Most evangelicals stayed inside denominations. In fact, as I will discuss below, most were housed within a single denomination. Although some broke away and founded new, independent churches, the proportion who did so was much smaller than in the United States. And unlike their American neighbours, Canadian evangelicals were not separatist. They were engaged in service work, politics, and social justice projects.

Much of the difference was caused by one key decision made in the evangelical Christian community of Canada: the establishment of the United Church of Canada (UCC) in 1925. In this democratic decision, individual churches decided whether to join together in one large denomination. Canadian evangelicals thus took a different path from American evangelicals. In the vote, all Methodists, almost all Presbyterians, and the Congregational Union of independent evangelical churches decided to unify rather than fracture (Eddy 1963). Thus, the UCC was established, becoming the third most populous denomination in Canada, behind the Catholic Church and the Anglican Church of Canada. In terms of historical institutionalist theory, this was a critical juncture in the historical paths taken by evangelical Christian communities in Canada and the United States.

The establishment of the UCC in 1925 had important effects on Canadian evangelicalism's capacity, decades later, to support the religious right movement. First, it affected the culture of Canadian evangelicalism (Bean 2014). Second, the shift reduced the number of conservative, evangelical Christians in Canada by nudging evangelicals toward the left and toward modernism. Third, it suppressed the organizational growth of parachurch organizations, which are an important part of the institutional infrastructure of the religious right movement.

The UCC scooped up the great majority of evangelical Christian Canadians. The census of Canada gives us a sense of the scope of the UCC's influence. It reports that in 1931, over 2 million Canadians were affiliated with the UCC, while less than seven percent of Canadians—about 670,000 individuals—were affiliated with evangelical churches other than the UCC (Canada Year Book 1967). Christianity in Canada at this time was "less fragmented, ... more ecumenical, and less prone to separate evangelical theology from social outreach" compared to the United States (Noll 1992). This fact is especially important because of the UCC's cultural impact on its congregants. Over the first four decades of its existence, the UCC nudged its congregation first toward a left-wing version of evangelicalism, and then out of evangelicalism altogether by formally adopting a modernist theology.

If you are familiar with the UCC today, it may be puzzling that I have thus far referred to it as an evangelical congregation, because it is not one today. The UCC is now widely seen as a very liberal, modernist denomination. But in 1925, when it was formed, it was an evangelical church. The church adhered to biblical literalism, and its worship practices had many of the features associated with evangelicalism, including evangelizing in the larger community. However, because it brought together people of diverse religious practices, from the outset the UCC established an ecumenical version of evangelicalism that allowed for a breadth of interpretation on some matters (for example, dispensationalism), but was very clear on its adherence to key tenets of evangelicalism, such as biblical inerrancy (Chown 1930). In the 1920s and 1930s, the UCC embraced an evangelical practice of religion that included revivals and a focus on personal salvation. Many leaders of the church were more modernist in their theology than the laity, but (in what some might characterize as a highly Canadian move) they simply avoided discussing these differences during worship and Sunday School. Historian Kevin Flatt (2013) describes the early UCC approach as "a 'quiet' modernism that avoided affirming evangelical doctrines though generally without repudiating them in public statements." According to Flatt, these "quiet" modern beliefs were coupled with "loud" evangelical practices that nudged the large evangelical flock toward modernist beliefs slowly over several decades, until the denomination formally shifted into modernism in the 1960s.

Part of the practice of evangelicalism that was important to UCC followers was its emphasis on social service. Evangelizing is central to many evangelical communities—establishing connections with outsiders whose souls might be saved. In many cases, evangelizing takes the form of street-corner education or door-knocking, but in Canada, the UCC established a vision of social service that was central to its evangelical commitments. The UCC was a key player in providing social services to people in hard times, throughout the Depression and up to the present (Christie and Gavreau 1996). Distinct from American evangelicals who were committed to separatism from the secular world, evangelicals in the UCC saw providing to the larger community as part of their mission. They forged ties to other institutions, such as universities, and were influential in establishing social work as a field of study (Christie and Gauvreau 1996). These priorities nudged followers to the left, creating a vision for a liberal evangelical Christianity. By the end of the 1960s, church leaders asserted a modern theology for the UCC as well by formally changing the Sunday School curriculum (Flatt 2013). While this move was controversial, as many churchgoers retained their biblical, literalist beliefs, the modernists won the day, and the UCC moved out of evangelicalism altogether.

The move toward liberal evangelicalism and then out of evangelicalism had a profound effect on the size of the conservative, evangelical Christian community in Canada. To be clear, there are conservative, evangelical Christians in Canada. Some evangelical churches did not join the UCC and carried on outside the UCC umbrella. However, by recruiting such a large proportion of evangelicals into their denomination and leading them out of evangelicalism, the UCC had an important effect on Canada's religious landscape. By the most generous estimates, provided by the Evangelical Foundation of Canada, ten percent of Canadians are evangelical at heart, if not in the pews today. The best estimates suggest that about five percent of Canadians were evangelical by the 1990s (Hiemstra 2008). In the United States, fully 41 percent of adults report being "born again or evangelical Christian" (Newport and Carroll 2005).

The UCC had another important effect apart from limiting the size of Canada's evangelical population. The UCC also suppressed the growth of the parachurch organizational sector by reducing the entrepreneurial opportunities for Canadian evangelicals to market to evangelical families. As the establishment of the UCC provided large numbers of Canadian evangelicals with a denominational home, it offered them the usual denominational supports and provisions. For example, the UCC offered Sunday School for children, social activities for families, community outreach, and social services. While this may not seem remarkable, it is relevant because, in the United States, evangelicals developed parachurch organizations to provide for every need of evangelicals, establishing a market-based way to create community.

In the United States, parachurch organizations are so dominant that they are understood to define the landscape of evangelicalism. As American evangelicals fractured and separated from the secular institutions and communities of non-evangelicals, a whole ecosystem of parachurch organizations emerged to supply all the goods and services that denominations usually supply. This ecosystem included printing presses that sold evangelical Christian books and magazines, home-school curricula for the education of children outside public schools, youth camps and other organizations that provided services to young people, and missionary travel programs that independent churches could align with to support the evangelical work of their congregants. American evangelical organizations were both for-profit and non-profit.

The growth of a large, parachurch organizational infrastructure in the United States fostered the separatism of American evangelicals not only by creating alternatives to secular institutions, but also by creating a subculture that could exist apart from the mainstream. Because they served evangelicals across churches and denominations, these parachurch organizations were fundamental to building a unifying, coherent "Christian" identity that signaled to evangelicals that they were in same camp, thus minimizing differences between churches. Collective identity is important to social movements, but in this case, before a social movement had emerged, the collective identity was being deployed in the market, not the political sphere. Many parachurch organizations in the United States were highly profitable, and this too, nourished the conservative, evangelical Christian community in the United States. Working within market logics, owners of parachurch organizations reinvested their profits in their businesses and marketed their goods to expand their consumer base.

Critical juncture 2: The regulation of religious broadcasting

Some profitable companies become large. This is particularly true of media companies, which brings us to the second critical juncture that pushed Canadian evangelicals off the American path: the Canadian government decided to regulate religious broadcasting in the early days of radio. In 1929, the Canadian government published the *Aird Report* (Aird et al. 1929), which is widely known for establishing public broadcasting in Canada. Indeed, Canada claimed the newly discovered airwaves as a public good, protecting them from market forces and placing the strong hand of government in charge of them through a licensing system.

At the same time, it established strict regulations on the content of religious radio broadcasts. Specifically, the *Aird Report* (1929) recommended "prohibiting statements of a controversial nature." The report further suggested that "competent and cultured announcers only should be employed." Perhaps most importantly, the Aird report restricted the profitability of radio by prohibiting most forms of advertising, including the ability to solicit donations from listeners. With these recommendations in hand, the government adopted policies to intervene directly in the character of Canadian culture. Unlike the United States (and in contrast to the fledgling evangelical radio programs that had begun to emerge across Canada), Canadian public discourse would be cultured and non-controversial. The ability to withhold broadcasting licenses would ensure adherence to these conventions. With a seemingly minor bureaucratic intervention, the Canadian government had a massive impact on Canada's cultural landscape.

This situation contrasted sharply with that of evangelical broadcasting in the United States, where the government took a *laissez-faire* approach to regulating broadcasting, and free speech reigned. Radio personalities could say anything they wanted, whether true or not. The more outlandish, the more popular and profitable their broadcasts would be. Perhaps that is why evangelical Christian broadcasts quickly became more popular than mainline Protestant broadcasts. When mainline churches colluded to squeeze evangelicals out of radio networks, evangelicals invented syndication (Finke and Stark 2005). Several evangelical broadcasters began making tapes of their programs and mailing them directly to independent radio stations across the country, bypassing network gatekeepers.

The success of market-based evangelical Christian radio in the United States produced some of the biggest and richest evangelical organizations in the world. Early radio broadcasters like Aimee Semple McPherson raised enough money broadcasting from her tent revival ministry to establish one of the first Pentecostal megachurches in the country at a cost of $1.5 million in 1923 (Ellens 1974). Some of them, like Charles Fuller, whose *Old-Fashioned Revival Hour* reached 20 million listeners, became household names (Schultze 1990). When television was invented, evangelical radio broadcasters turned to televangelism, while Canadian TV broadcasts were heavily regulated by the same policies that governed radio. Meanwhile, American evangelical media organizations proliferated, grew, and profited. Bob Jones, Sr., a radio broadcaster for 35 years, founded Bob Jones College (now University), an evangelical postsecondary institution that claims to train leaders for the evangelical community and runs a program that teaches evangelical broadcasting to students. Billy Graham's Evangelical Association founded a media empire that publishes *Christianity Today,* considered evangelicalism's flagship magazine. Liberty University, run by Jerry Falwell, Jr., was funded by his father's televangelism enterprise.

For American evangelicals, religious broadcasting produced massive profits. Finke and Stark (2005) report that evangelicals were by far the most profitable radio broadcasters. Their television broadcasts were similarly profitable. In contrast, for conservative evangelicals in Canada, radio was something one had to raise money to pay for. For example, T.T. Shields started a radio program affiliated with his Toronto Baptist Seminary, but it failed because it could not keep up with production costs (Johnston 1994). William ("Bible Bill") Aberhart, who got his start in radio before the *Aird Report*, was able to make some money from his "radio clubs" and build a $50,000 extension for his Bible Institute, but when the restrictive regulations were put into place, the profitability of his radio broadcasts fell (Johnson and MacNutt 1970).

The effect on the Canadian conservative, evangelical Christian community

In the 1980s, the religious right emerged as a social movement in Canada and the United States, but the movements did not rest on equally supportive institutional foundations. In Canada, the political party that Aberhart built was alive and well as the Reform Party. It offered a platform for conservative, evangelical Christian Canadians in the political sphere, and was one minority voice among many in a diverse political spectrum. In the United States, evangelicals flooded into the political sphere, forming a large voting bloc that shifted American politics dramatically toward social conservatism. The movement relied on a well-resourced set of networked organizations, as well as a rich media landscape that came with millions of supporters and their own TV programs, their own television channels, their own radio networks, and a network of churches and people who shared a collective identity. While the institutional infrastructure of Canada's religious right allows the movement to exist, it does not dominate the political landscape the way its American counterpart does. My research reveals the role that two Canadian choices—the formation of the UCC and the regulation of radio broadcasting— played in influencing the opportunities that right-wing activists faced when they established their movements in each country.

For social movement theorists, this research produces instructive insights. First, social movements don't simply diffuse—or at least, don't diffuse simply—across national borders and cultural contexts, even for countries as similar and as closely connected as the United States and Canada. This finding joins insights developed by others (e.g., Wood 2012), who are working to understand barriers to diffusion of justice- and equality-oriented movements. To this project, my research adds an important directive: to understand movements over their lifetime, look historically at the political and cultural conditions prior to movement emergence.

How should we think about policy, culture, and right-wing activism today?

Today, right-wing populism is surging. Although not totally disentangled from the cultural and organizational bases of the religious right, these new forms of right-wing activism do not articulate their social change positions in terms of an evangelical Christian theology or, for the most part, rely on the religious right's organizational base. Rather than religion, what ties these populists together is a desire to see traditional white masculinity reasserted as superior to other identity categories, and to see the social positions of white men become even more culturally and structurally dominant.

There are two main types of leader in this right-wing push. Most visible are the political figures who have risen to power through electoral politics. This includes President Trump in the United States and Ontario Premier Doug Ford in Canada, as well as figures across the globe who stoke populist fears and use racial tropes to garner mass support for authoritarian and isolationist political strategies. The second type consists of cultural entrepreneurs, who elevate their fame and accumulate riches by rallying supporters to their white masculinist causes. Here I have in mind provocateurs like Milo Yiannapolis, Richard Spencer, and Jordan Peterson, but also established veterans of the old-media outrage industry like Rush Limbaugh, Alex Jones, and Ann Coulter (Berry and Sobieraj 2016).

Although we might like to think of these mainly American entrepreneurs as extreme, it is important to keep in mind that mainstream Canadian culture also places a high value on white masculinity. Our dominant cultural imaginary of a "real" Canadian is a man playing hockey on a lake, wearing an ear-flap toque and a red plaid coat. He is working-class, perhaps drinking beer from the two-four that he picked up at the Beer Store. This is how we picture real Canadians, even though 80 percent of Canadians live in or around cities, half of us are women, almost a quarter of us are members of visible minority groups, and 95 percent of us are colonial settlers occupying the lands of Indigenous peoples who were here long before this country was named Canada. White masculinity is culturally central, even in our multicultural landscape.

Its cultural centrality is supported by a system of inequality in which white men are overrepresented in positions of power in government, business, bureaucracies, and in decision-making positions in most workplaces. These inequalities are evident in measures of income inequality, occupational status, incarceration rates, and measures of representation in electoral politics. Although our cultural tropes of multiculturalism and gender equality might convince many of us otherwise, structural equality has not been achieved for Black or Indigenous people, visible minority groups, or women of any ethnicity. Thus, it should not surprise us that right-wing ideologies, and especially white masculinist ideologies, are popular here as well as in the United States and parts of Europe where populism has been ascendant.

The popularity of white masculinist ideologies in Canada is not the same as right-wing movements being on the rise. As I have discussed, a strong movement needs more than just an idea; it requires an organizational infrastructure, as well as cultural supports like a collective identity and a way to talk about issues that inspires potential recruits. It is important in this regard to keep in mind the difference between how easy it is for ideas to travel across national borders compared to the people, organizations, money and cultural apparatus that turn ideas into a strong social movement. Right-wing entrepreneurs use a variety of platforms in both traditional and new media to inspire large followings. Although the extent to which their explicit comments are racist and sexist varies, their overall message opposes any social change that values equality and multiculturalism.

It is necessary to come to terms with the fact that right-wing ideology forms an important part of the Canadian cultural landscape. It is easy to find, and a sizable number of people find the ideology appealing, even some women and people of colour. Its message is supported by a cultural infrastructure of radio, television, and print sources that attract reliable but modest-sized audiences. On the other hand, Internet forums, chat rooms, discussion boards, YouTube channels, and Patreon support accounts suggest the existence of an energetic and possibly growing online community—or set of communities—supporting various flavours of the white-masculinity message. However, measures of audience size in the new media are imprecise, and their potential to produce social change is uncertain (for example, it is unclear what proportion of these viewers are also members of the Canadian electorate). It is perhaps telling, however, that Faith Goldy, a white supremacist candidate for mayor in the 2018 Toronto election, won about 3 percent of the popular vote, attracting around 1 percent of eligible voters.

Social movement scholarship suggests that organizational strength, financial resources, and the size of the audience base for white masculinist messaging are keys to understanding the potential for social change that goes beyond the free exchange of ideas in the public square to policy changes, increased tolerance for violence against marginalized people, and the election of white masculinist governments. These are the factors that we must investigate to learn about the potential of the new cast of right-wing characters in the public sphere today.

What lessons can we derive from the foregoing analysis? Principally, I think, that we need to be thoughtful and principled about the decisions we make today because they could easily have important ramifications in the future. Canada's longstanding approach to controversial issues has been to exert bureaucratic control to limit the influence of extreme views and downplay conflicts in public debate. We might apply these principles to contemporary issues. Consider the example of Ontario's recent requirement that universities establish free-speech policies for their campuses. On the face of it, the idea seems harmless enough. Who is against free speech, especially on a university campus? We imagine a well-intentioned exchange of ideas, decry censorship, and think that fair-minded debate will sort the good ideas from the harmful ones. This may be true. However, looking back to 1929, it is not how Canadian bureaucrats saw the situation in the early days of radio when they insisted that the content be civil and non-controversial. They argued that debate should be characterized by decorum and little if any market influence. A similar policy example is Canada's approach to hate speech, which holds that promotion of hatred or advocacy of genocide is not protected free speech. Canadians, unlike their American neighbours, have decided they want a limit on free speech for the greater good—what the British North America Act calls "peace, order, and good government."

If universities adhere to the Ontario government's directive, we offer up our universities as places that are required to feature speakers with extreme right-wing views. This may not be a problem. As long as an idea lacks an organized, resource-rich, institutional infrastructure to help turn it into practice, there is no harm in considering it, especially when logic and evidence is allowed to deal with it. However, if the white masculinist idea enjoys considerable organized support, the policy change that universities are being asked to undertake today might one day have dangerous consequences. A large pool of external funds routinely supporting professional right-wing speakers, conferences, rallies, and publications, could wear out the pool of poorly resourced volunteer experts to debate and tackle their ideas on their merits. External funding for the propagation of right-wing ideas is not a possibility that we have fully considered as university administrators strike committees to write up free speech policies. My research on right-wing activism in Canada suggests that this concern should be at the forefront of our debates about free speech policy.

It is important to apply a comparative lens when thinking about how Canada wants to address its policy choices today. Fortunately, we always have the United States to offer an example of unimpeded free speech and unregulated, market-driven cultural institutions. If Canada decides to become more like the United States, we know what policies to change, and we can see what the expected results might look like. If, on the other hand, Canada would like to take a different path, it will be instructive to look at our own historic bureaucratic and cultural actions. We may want to place reasonable limits on the kinds of speech we allow on university campuses, perhaps by referring to hate crime law, so that our public discourse can address the important issues of the day without signing over a public good like our university campuses to social movement actors with a propensity to make false claims for divisive ends. Whichever choice Canada makes, historical institutionalism reminds us that the choices that we make today can be of crucial importance in the future.

References

Aird, John, Charles A. Bowman, and Augustin Frigon. 1929. *Report of the Royal Commission on Radio Broadcasting [The Aird Commission Report]*. Ottawa: Royal Commission on Radio Broadcasting.

Bean, Lydia. 2014. *The Politics of Evangelical Identity: Local Churches and Partisan Divides in the United States and Canada*. Princeton, NJ: Princeton University Press.

Berry, Jeffrey M. and Sarah Sobieraj. 2016. *The Outrage Industry: Political Opinion Media and the New Incivility*. New York: Oxford University Press.

Canada Year Book. 1967. *Canada Year Book: 1948–49*. Ottawa: Dominion Bureau of Statistics.

Capoccia, Giovanni and R. Daniel Kelemen. 2007. The study of critical junctures: Theory, narrative, and counterfactuals in historical institutionalism. *World Politics* 59(3): 341–69.

Chown, Samuel Dwight. 1930. *The Story of Church Union in Canada*. Toronto: Ryerson Press.

Christie, Nancy and Michael Gauvreau. 1996. *A Full-Orbed Christianity: The Protestant Churches and Social Welfare in Canada, 1900–1940*. Montreal and Kingston: McGill-Queen's University Press.

Desai, Manisha. 1996. Informal organizations as agents of change: Notes from the contemporary women's movement in India. *Mobilization: An International Quarterly* 1(2): 159–73.

Eddy, Earl B. 1963. The Congregational tradition. Pp. 25–37 in *The Churches and the Canadian Experience: A Faith and Order Study of the Christian Tradition, World Council of Churches Theological Study Commission on Tradition and Traditions*, edited by J. W. Grant. Toronto: Ryerson Press.

Elliott, David Raymond and Iris Miller. 1987. *Bible Bill: A Biography of William Aberhart*. Edmonton, AB: Reidmore Books.

Fetner, Tina. Forthcoming. The religious right in the United States and Canada: Evangelical communities, critical junctures, and institutional infrastructures. *Mobilization: An International Quarterly*.

Finke, Roger and Rodney Stark. 2005. *The Churching of America, 1776–2005: Winners and Losers in Our Religious Economy*. New Brunswick, NJ: Rutgers University Press.

Flatt, Kevin N. 2013. *After Evangelicalism: The Sixties and the United Church of Canada*. Montreal: McGill-Queen's University Press.

Hiemstra, Rick. 2008. Evangelicals and the Canadian census. *Church and Faith Trends: A Publication of The Centre for Research on Canadian Evangelicalism* 1(2): 1–13.

Johnson, LeRoy Peter Vernon and Ola J. MacNutt. 1970. *Aberhart of Alberta*. Edmonton, AB: Co-op Press.

McCarthy, John D. and Mayer N. Zald. 1977. Resource mobilization and social movements: A partial theory. *American Journal of Sociology* 82(6): 1212–41.

Morris, Aldon. 1984. *The Origins of the Civil Rights Movement: Black Communities Organizing for Change.* New York: Free Press.

Newport, Frank and Joseph Carroll. 2005. Another look at evangelicals in America today. *Gallup News Service*, December 2.

Noll, Mark A. 1992. *A History of Christianity in the United States and Canada.* Grand Rapids, MI: W.B. Eerdmans.

Pierson, Paul and Theda Skocpol. 2002. Historical institutionalism in contemporary political science. Pp. 693–721 in *Political Science: The State of the Discipline*, edited by I. Katznelson and H. Milner. New York: Norton.

Schultze, Quentin J. 1990. The invisible medium: Evangelical radio. Pp. 171–95 in *American Evangelicals and the Mass Media: Perspectives on the Relationship between American Evangelicals and the Mass Media*, edited by Q. J. Schultze. Grand Rapids, MI: Zondervan Corp.

Slavina, Anna, and Robert Brym. 2019. Demonstrating in the Internet age: A test of Castells' theory. *Social Movement Studies* 20 (3).

Smith, Christian. 1998. *American Evangelicalism: Embattled and Thriving.* Chicago: University of Chicago Press.

Wood, Lesley J. 2012. *Direct Action, Deliberation, and Diffusion: Collective Action after the WTO Protests in Seattle.* Cambridge, UK: Cambridge University Press.

CHAPTER SIX
The Macro Context of Critical Events and Meso-Level Connectivity

Anna Slavina

The election of Donald Trump, the Women's March following his inauguration, increased protest at both ends of the political spectrum, and the proliferation of social media as tools for political mobilization and repression have led many social movement analysts to argue that the current political moment is characterized by change in how states and citizens engage in politics. However, the durable effects of the ongoing tumult are uncertain. To make sense of them, the contributors to this volume highlight the role of critical events in triggering change in the relationship between state and society, with implications for the forms that social movements assume.

However, critical events and the transformation of institutional relationships take place in a larger social context. Macro-level factors such as national political culture and political economy influence the development and structure of social movements. A well-rounded theory of contemporary social movements must knit together micro, meso, and macro levels of analysis by situating critical events and institutional relationships in broader national and cross-national contexts and trends.

This is not a novel idea. Tilly (2006) shows how the structure and repertoires of social movements, as well as movements' relationships with the state and civil society, are conditioned by macro-level political and economic structures inscribed in national regimes. Bourdieu (1984; 1990) argues that, to interact and compete for power, actors need to know the rules of the game governing a field and follow complementary schemas of action and communication. Both scholars would agree that micro-level processes and meso-level relationships between social movements, political institutions, and the state rest on macro-level foundations. As the foundations shift, social movement forms change. Such change is usually gradual because, as Bourdieu (1984) emphasizes, the structure of fields and the dispositions of actors contribute to the stability and reproduction of social relationships; characteristically, Tilly's (1995) analysis of social movement development in Britain spans seven decades.

Despite the typically slow pace of change, Manuel Castells (2012 [2015]), among others, argued just a few years ago that the development of online social networking had quickly revolutionized contemporary activism, allowing protest to spread across the world by contagion. We now know that many if not most online social movements tend to dissipate as quickly as they form, and their lasting effects are unclear (Slavina and Brym 2019). Castells' hurried conclusion teaches us that, while critical events have the potential to trigger social change, not all events that create opportunities for movement activism have the potential to reorder institutions, social relations, and power (Ramos 2008). How then should we view the role of critical events in affecting institutional relationships?

In this volume, Ramos proposes field theory as a promising avenue of research. Bourdieu (1985) defines fields as sites of "struggle over the definition of the legitimate principles of the division of the field." Actors in fields compete over the power relations that link them and the rules of the game that guide their actions. According to Ramos and Wood (in this volume), critical events can disrupt power relations and taken-for-granted understandings in fields, thus contributing to social change.

Field theory's relational focus makes it particularly useful for understanding how shifts in power relations lead to the legitimization of discourses, frames, and political repertoires. For example, Indigenous Canadians struggled to win the constitutionally protected right to be consulted on matters that affect them. The "duty to consult" recently gave Indigenous activists an edge by allowing them to at least temporarily halt the construction of the Trans Mountain pipeline.

However, those who wish to apply field theory need to keep in mind that some sites and relationships within fields are susceptible to rapid change while others contribute to stability and reproduction. As Bourdieu (1984) notes, status differences, hierarchies, and power relations are justified by unconscious behaviours and inscribed in the structure of institutions. Inequality is typically maintained because those with the most power enjoy the capacity to define structures and narratives to their advantage. Thus, although the explosion of social media networking at first appeared to disrupt power inequalities between activists and states by lowering the cost of mobilization and network building, the concentration of economic, cultural, informational, and symbolic power meant that governments and upper classes were soon able to monitor the Internet and/or control it to their advantage (Brym et al. 2018). As Ramos notes, Trump's Make America Great Again campaign even borrowed strategies and narratives from the repertoires of traditional social movements to consolidate power. Similarly, we can see how the structure of a field contributes to the maintenance of unequal power relations between elites and the public in Wood's description of how some states have sidelined consultation with minority groups. In short, progressive change can becomes inscribed in structures, thus helping to maintain hard-won safeguards against the abuse of power, but regressive change has the same or greater potential.

If Ramos's and Wood's chapters suggest the need to analyze the sources of variation in the durability of micro-level sites and relationships within fields, Corrigall-Brown's and Fetner's chapters recommend meso-level analyses of institutional relationships to better understand how social movements develop or fail to do so.

Fetner argues that the religious right in the United States is much stronger than its Canadian counterpart for two reasons. First, the 1925 unification of nearly all evangelical churches in Canada led to the development of an organization that was scarcely different from mainline churches. In contrast, the absence of unification allowed various hardline evangelical factions to proliferate in the United States. Second, the Canadian government's 1929 limitation on religious broadcasting prevented extreme factions of the evangelical movement from spreading their message. Meanwhile, the relative lack of government control over the content of broadcasting in the United States permitted evangelical factions to popularize their gospel. According to Fetner, the presence or absence of such institutional brakes accounts for differences in the success of the evangelical movement in the United States and Canada and, consequently, the ability of right-wing religious social movements in the United States to harness the resources, networks, and media presence of powerful church organizations. Also drawing on institutional analysis, Corrigall-Brown shows that, in the year following Trump's election, even some conservative American cities managed to spawn Indivisible groups that sustained activism. This feat was possible where the groups invested resources to build relationships with other civic organizations and mechanisms for lowering the cost associated with activism. Failure to construct such institutional scaffolding meant that Indivisible groups were short-lived.

If the contributors to this volume usefully highlight how micro-level critical events in fields and meso-level patterns of institutional connectivity can help movements endure, they miss the opportunity to identify how micro-, meso-, and macro-level processes are linked. The importance of drawing this connection may be appreciated by returning to Fetner's example.

The kind of institutional oligopolization and government intervention that Fetner identifies are near-constant themes in Canadian history and are grounded in its political economy. As Harold Innis 1930 [1999] established, the vastness of the country and its relatively inhospitable geography and climate made it necessary for governments to take a strong hand in facilitating economic development. Thus, in 1670, King Charles II granted a trading monopoly over one-third of what is now Canada to the Hudson's Bay Company. Analgously, just six banks control approximately 90 percent of domestic bank assets (Allen and Liu 2007). Broadcasting policy followed a similar trajectory; in 1932, R.B. Bennett, Canada's 11th Prime Minister, stated that without complete government control of broadcasting, radio "could never become the agency by which national consciousness may be fostered and national unity … strengthened" (quoted in Competition Bureau 2002). These examples suggest that Canada's relatively small population, low population density, and scarce resources and personnel made organizational diversity difficult to achieve. The growth of a near-monopolistic evangelical church in Canada was homologous with the growth of other Canadian institutions because it was grounded in the same political-economic context.

The Canadian government's culture of top-down policy regulation continues to shape legislation that affects meso-level relationships among social movements, religious organizations, and other civil society groups. For instance, the Canadian government recently stipulated that organizations wanting to qualify for student grants through the Summer Jobs Program must sign an attestation that the organization's core mandate supports human rights, including reproductive rights and freedom from discrimination based on sexual orientation and gender identity and expression. The policy makes it difficult for any organization to support or affiliate with a church or group supporting anti-abortion initiatives or to form relationships with social movements on the religious right. This remains the case even after the language of the regulation was watered down following protests by the Catholic Church (Platt 2018). In contrast, in the United States, a political culture emphasizing pluralism and a free market of voluntary associations makes the adoption of such policies highly unlikely (Warner 1993).

As the example of the religious right shows, differences between macro-level contexts matter. They likely account for variation in the incidence of critical events and the likelihood that particular institutional patterns will exert an enduring impact on the form and impact of social movements. As such, they demand our sustained attention.

References

Allen, J. and Y. Liu. 2007. Efficiency and economies of scale of large Canadian banks. *Canadian Journal of Economics* 40(1): 225–244.

Bourdieu, P. 1990. *The Logic of Practice.* Stanford, CA: Stanford University Press.

Bourdieu, P. 1985. The social space and the genesis of groups. *Theory and Society* 14(6): 723–44.

Bourdieu, P. 1984. *Distinction: A Social Critique of the Judgement of Taste.* Cambridge, MA: Harvard University Press.

Brym, R., A. Slavina, M. Todosijevic, and D. Cowan. 2018. Social movement horizontality in the Internet age? A critique of Castells in light of the Trump victory. *Canadian Review of Sociology* 55(4): 624–34.

Castells, M. 2012 [2015]. *Networks of Outrage and Hope: Social Movements in the Internet Age*, 2nd ed. Cambridge, UK: Polity.

Competition Bureau. 2002. Comments of the Commissioner of Competition to the Standing Committee on Canadian Heritage on the Study of the State of the Canadian Broadcasting System. Ottawa: Government of Canada.

Innis, H.A. 1930 [1999]. *The Fur Trade in Canada: An Introduction to Canadian Economic History.* Toronto: University of Toronto Press.

Platt, B. 2018a. Faith groups among those out millions in summer jobs funding after refusing to sign attestation to respect abortion rights. *National Post*, 16 March. https://nationalpost.com/news/politics/groups-scramble-for-replacement-funding-after-dissenting-on-canada-summer-jobs-abortion-attestation.

Platt, B. 2018b. "The values test is gone": Faith groups welcome changes to summer jobs attestation. *National Post*, 7 December. https://nationalpost.com/news/politics/here-is-what-the-new-canada-summer-jobs-attestation-says.

Ramos, H. 2008. Opportunity for whom? Political opportunity and critical events in Canadian Aboriginal mobilization, 1951–2000. *Social Forces* 87(2): 795–824.

Slavina, Anna, and Robert Brym. 2019. Demonstrating in the Internet age: A test of Castells' theory. *Social Movement Studies* 20(3).

Tilly, C. 2006. *Regimes and Repertoires.* Chicago: University of Chicago Press.

Tilly, C. 1995. *Popular Contention in Great Britain, 1758–1834.* Cambridge, MA: Harvard University Press.

Warner, S.R. 1993. Work in progress: Toward a new paradigm for the sociological study of religion in the United States. *American Journal of Sociology* 98(5): 1044–93.

Contributors

Robert Brym is S.D. Clark Professor of Sociology at the University of Toronto and a Fellow of the Royal Society of Canada. He has won numerous awards for his research and teaching and has published internationally on politics and ethnic relations in Russia, the Middle East, and Canada. For details and downloadable publications, visit https://utoronto.academia.edu/RobertBrym.

Catherine Corrigall-Brown is Associate Professor in the Department of Sociology, University of British Columbia. Her research focuses on participation in social movements. Her first book, *Patterns of Protest* (Stanford University Press, 2011), analyzes individual trajectories of participation of activism over the life course. Her research has appeared in *Social Forces, Mobilization,* the *Canadian Review of Sociology,* and *Sociological Perspectives.* She is the winner of the Canadian Sociological Association Early Investigator Award.

Tina Fetner is Associate Professor of Sociology at McMaster University. Her research examines LGBT activism, anti-LGBT activism, and social and political change around sexuality. Her research projects include analyses of change in attitudes toward lesbian and gay people, and the uneven growth of supports for youth, such as Gay-Straight Alliances. Her most recent project examines the social organization of sexual behaviour and its intersection with social and political attitudes.

Howard Ramos is Professor of Sociology and Associate Dean of Research, Faculty of Arts and Social Science, Dalhousie University, Halifax, Nova Scotia. He has published widely on social movements, human rights, race, and immigration. For details and downloadable publications, visit http://howardramos.ca/ and http://perceptionsofchange.ca.

Anna Slavina is a doctoral candidate in the Department of Sociology at the University of Toronto. Her research uses survey data to examine cultures of political activism, showing how different forms of political engagement cluster into nationally distinct repertoires that share regional similarities; and how the meaning of political action is culturally and structurally rooted in identifiable social contexts and individuals' experiences. Her work has been published in the *Canadian Review of Sociology, Social Movement Studies,* and as chapters in edited volumes.

Lesley J. Wood is Associate Professor and Chair of the Department of Sociology at York University in Toronto. She studies contentious politics, particularly repression, temporal dynamics, and solidarity. Her *Direct Action, Deliberation, and Diffusion: Collective Action after the WTO Protests in Seattle* (Cambridge University Press, 2012) won the John Porter Award of the Canadian Sociological Association. Her publications and more information about her research can be found at http://profiles.laps.yorku.ca/profiles/ljwood/.

Index

Proceedings of the S.D. Clark Symposium on the Future of Canadian Society

OTHER VOLUMES IN THE SERIES

The Future of Canada's Territorial Borders and Personal Boundaries:
Proceedings of the Third Symposium
Canadian identity, governmentality, and security are affected by both the permeability and the strengthening of national borders and personal boundaries. In this symposium, leading figures in the study of borders and boundaries analyze and debate the contested Arctic, the securitization of the Canada/U.S. border, and the Internet's threat to personal sovereignty. Contributors include John Hannigan, Ronald J. Deibert, Heather N. Nicol, Klaus Dodds, Louis W. Pauly, and Emily Gilbert.

Immigration and the Future of Canadian Society:
Proceedings of the Second Symposium
"A spectre is haunting Europe and the United States—the spectre of immigration." So begins Robert Brym's introduction to the second volume of proceedings of the annual S.D. Clark Symposium. Contributors Richard Alba, Jeffrey G. Reitz, Naomi Lightman, Monica Boyd, Patricia Landolt, and Salina Abji consider the social and political effects and implications of immigration, both from a comparative perspective and with a specific focus on the Canadian experience in the early years of the twenty-first century. The result is a thought-provoking examination of one of the most important issues of our time.

Inequality and the Future of Canadian Society:
Proceedings of the First Symposium
S.D. Clark, the first chair of the Department of Sociology at the University of Toronto, was one of Canada's leading sociologists in the middle years of the twentieth century. Late in his career, he conducted research on how economic change in Canada resulted in inequality as reflected in patterns of residential segregation. The first S.D. Clark Symposium picked up where Clark left off by focusing on income inequality and its implications. Contributors include Robert Andersen, Lars Osberg, Ito Peng, Gordon Cleveland, John Myles, and Emily Laxer, with Robert Brym's introduction providing an overview of the subject.

www.ingramcontent.com/pod-product-compliance
Lightning Source LLC
Chambersburg PA
CBHW051031030426
42336CB00015B/2821